From Great Paragraphs to Great Essays

From Great Paragraphs to Great Essays

Keith S. Folse
University of Central Florida

Elena Vestri Solomon
Hillsborough Community College

David Clabeaux
Hillsborough Community College

For teaching notes, answer key, and other related instructor material, as well as for additional student activities related to this book, go to college.hmco.com/pic/folseFGPGE1e.

To obtain access to the Houghton Mifflin ESL instructor sites, call 1-800-733-1717.

Houghton Mifflin Company
Boston New York

Publisher: Patricia A. Coryell
Editor in Chief: Suzanne Phelps Weir
Sponsoring Editor: Joann Kozyrev
Senior Development Editor: Kathleen Sands-Boehmer
Development Editor: Kathleen M. Smith
Editorial Assistant: Evangeline Bermas
Senior Project Editor: Margaret Park Bridges
Associate Manufacturing Buyer: Brian Pieragostini
Executive Marketing Manager: Annamarie Rice
Marketing Assistant: Andrew Whitacre

Cover image: Gears © 2000 Lisa Zador/Artville

Printed in the U.S.A.

Library of Congress Control Number: 2002109448

Student Text
    ISBN 13: 978-0-618-26537-4
    ISBN 10: 0-618-26537-6

Instructor's Examination Copy
    ISBN 13: 978-0-618-73345-3
    ISBN 10: 0-618-73345-0

23456789-CRS-10 09 08 07 06

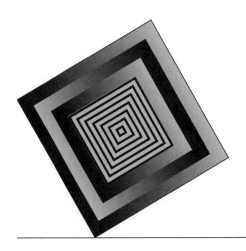

Contents

Unit 2 Five Elements of Good Writing 28

Unit 3 Types of Paragraphs 50

Unit 6 Cause-Effect Essays   116

Unit 7 Classification Essays   137

Substitve
Argumtstn

Appendix: Peer Editing Sheets   159

Index   189

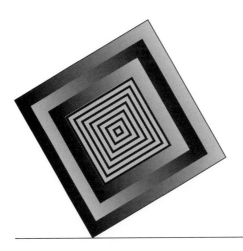

Overview

Composing paragraphs and essays involves both a process and a product. While teachers want to emphasize the process, students are rightfully concerned about their written products. For many students, not being able to write effectively and easily in English is a major obstacle to their educational plans. Therefore, the activities in this book deal with elements that affect the quality of a written product, including grammar, organization, and logic.

In *From Great Paragraphs to Great Essays*, we begin with the paragraph, show how paragraphs are similar to essays, and then introduce, examine, and develop essays. We have made every effort to include more than enough writing instruction and practice to eliminate the need for teachers to search for additional ancillary materials. To this end, this textbook contains 102 activities with 20 suggestions for additional essay assignments. There are 67 example paragraphs, more than half of them in eight example essays. In addition, supplementary activities are available on the accompanying website. We designed this book for intermediate students. Depending on the class level and the amount of writing that is done outside of class hours, there is enough material for 60 to 80 classroom hours. Provided that enough writing is done outside the classroom, the number of hours can be as few as 40. The best judge of which units and activities should be covered with any group of students is ALWAYS the teacher of that group. Therefore, it is up to you to gauge your students' needs and then match these needs with the book material.

TEXT ORGANIZATION

From Great Paragraphs to Great Essays consists of two parts. Units 1 to 3 work on the paragraph, while Units 4 to 7 work on the transition from paragraph writing to essay writing and on developing specific types of essays. The book ends with an appendix of Peer Editing Sheets.

TEACHING FROM THIS BOOK

There are as many ways to use *From Great Paragraphs to Great Essays* as there are composition teachers. We hope that the teaching material and the array of activities, tasks, and checklists will serve as a solid guide to help students navigate the writing of paragraphs and essays.

The units in this book can be used in any order. This is an extremely important point because schools have different writing curriculum plans. One logical order of using these units is in the existing numerical sequence with paragraphs first. Alternatively, if students are ready for essays, you could start with Units 4 to 7 and use Units 1 to 3 for follow-up review as needed. If students have a general idea of what a paragraph and an essay are, then you might concentrate on Unit 3 (types of paragraphs) and Units 5, 6, and 7 (essay types). You could cover a paragraph type from Unit 3 and then cover that same type of essay in a later unit. Regardless of which sequencing is chosen, we believe that most teachers will want to cover the Language Focus sections to help students become better self-editors, which is certainly a goal of a maturing writer.

Online Teaching Center

For the answer key, teaching notes, sample syllabi, and unit tests, visit the *From Great Paragraphs to Great Essays* instructor website: college.hmco.com/pic/folseFGPGE1e

Online Study Center

As with all of Houghton Mifflin's language textbooks, this book has an accompanying student website that is both fun and helpful for our students and enables them to practice and improve their writing skills. Some of the activities on the Online Study Center encourage students to use sentence type variety, and others provide students with the opportunity to become more comfortable using transitions for different rhetorical types. In addition, there are paragraph activities that help the students to practice coherence and unity. Some activities are designed to give students editing practice, and other exercises provide practice in recognizing common writing mistakes. Vocabulary activities help students to recognize meaning and correct part of speech usage. All of these activities plus the Peer Editing Sheets present opportunities for helpful feedback that will allow the students to work on their own. We hope that you will visit and use the website often at college.hmco.com/pic/folseFGPGE1e

ACKNOWLEDGMENTS

From Great Paragraphs to Great Essays is the result of the planning, input, and encouragement of a great many people. We are especially grateful to our editors at Houghton Mifflin, Susan Maguire and Kathy Sands-Boehmer, who were there for us time and time again as this book progressed. Susan had the vision and energy to get this project started, and Kathy had the fortitude and patience to make sure that we finished it. We are grateful to both for their part in this work.

We wish to express our immense gratitude to Kathleen Smith, our developmental editor, who so diligently helped us to incorporate reviewers' and teachers' suggestions into this work. This work would not be the work that it is without her indispensable and insightful editing.

We thank April Muchmore-Vokoun for her excellent work on the web activities.

We would also like to acknowledge the thousands of students that the three of us have taught over the years. Although it is impossible to single out one or two students, we realize that this book is the result of our interactions with our writing students from many classes over many years. As our students learned to improve their writing, we learned to improve our teaching methods and materials.

Finally, we thank these reviewers whose comments were instrumental in the development of *From Great Paragraphs to Great Essays:* Nancy Booth, Hudson County Community College; Charlotte Calobrisi, Northern Virginia Community College; Sherwin Kizner, LaGuardia Community College; Elis Lee, Glendale Community College; Michelle Munro, Suffolk Community College; Alan Schute, Bunker Hill Community College; and Christopher Wahl, Hudson County Community College.

Keith S. Folse

Elena Vestri Solomon

David Clabeaux

Introduction to Paragraphs

Writing Goal:	Understanding paragraph parts
Language Focus 1:	Identifying verbs and fragments
Language Focus 2:	Nouns and noun forms
Examples:	Paragraphs 1–9

DEFINITION: WHAT IS A PARAGRAPH?

A paragraph is a collection of sentences that describe, discuss, or explain one central idea. Generally, a paragraph is composed of one topic sentence and a number of other sentences that either support or describe the topic sentence. As you will learn later in this book, just as sentences can be combined into paragraphs, paragraphs can be combined into essays.

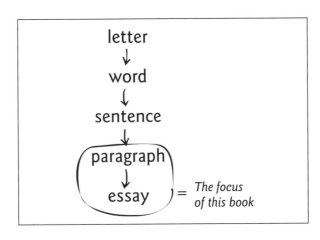

To better understand what a paragraph is, we must look at its individual parts. The three main parts of a paragraph are (1) the topic sentence, (2) the supporting detail sentences, and (3) the concluding sentence.

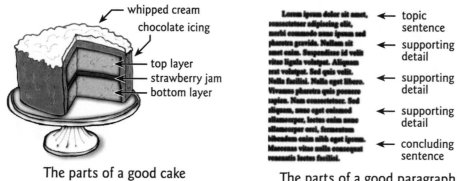

The parts of a good cake

The parts of a good paragraph

Think about a piece of cake. Although we think of a cake as one food, it is actually made up of different parts. No single part is the cake; it is a good cake only when it includes all of the parts in the right amount. As you read about the parts of a good paragraph, remember this simple analogy to the parts of a good cake.

Topic Sentences

A **topic sentence** tells the reader the main idea or thought that the writer is trying to convey. It is a one-sentence summary of the entire paragraph. Each sentence that follows helps to develop the idea presented in this topic sentence.

The organization of a paragraph is based on the topic sentence. Although it can be found in any part of the paragraph, the topic sentence is frequently the first sentence in the paragraph.

Elements of a Topic Sentence

The two main elements of a topic sentence are

- main subject
- controlling idea

A topic sentence contains the **main subject** of the paragraph and a **controlling idea**. The controlling idea steers the main topic in the direction that the writer wants. Study the following examples:

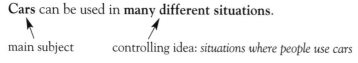

Cars can be used in **many different situations**.

main subject   controlling idea: *situations where people use cars*

In this sentence, we know that the paragraph is going to discuss something about cars (main subject). It will explain how people use cars in different ways (controlling idea).

Cars have **changed** enormously **in the past 50 years**.

main subject   controlling idea: *the change of cars over time*

In this sentence, we know that the paragraph is going to explain how cars have changed over time.

Different **cars** can **appeal** to **different people**.

main subject   controlling idea: *list cars that different people like*

Here, we know that the paragraph is going to explain how different kinds of people like different cars.

Now look at the next example:

Cars were invented in the 20th century.

main subject

In this sentence, the information is a simple fact. There is not a good controlling idea that a writer can discuss in a paragraph. This is not a good topic sentence because there is no indication of anything more to say about the topic.

Activity 1   **Selecting a Good Topic Sentence**

In each pair, choose the better topic sentence. Be prepared to explain your choices.

1. _____ a. Bilingual dictionaries can help nonnative learners in two very important ways.

   _____ b. In a bilingual dictionary, the information is presented in two different languages.

2. _____ a. An accused person has to appear in court as part of a successful trial process.

   _____ b. An accused person must do three important things to ensure a successful trial.

3. _____ a. Fossils are the remains of plants or animals that died a long time ago.

   _____ b. There are three techniques that scientists use to discover the true age of a fossil.

4. _____ a. Computers have changed people's communication patterns.

_____ b. Computers are expensive.

5. _____ a. Dogs have very specific traits that make them a popular pet.

_____ b. Chihuahuas, poodles, German shepherds, terriers, and beagles are popular pets.

Activity 2 | Studying Topic Sentences in a Paragraph

Read and study the following process paragraph. Answer the questions.

Paragraph 1 (process)

The topic of this paragraph is how to change a flat tire. It is a simple process, but many people have a difficult time completing this procedure.

Before you read the paragraph, discuss these questions with your classmates.

1. Have you ever had a flat tire on your car? _____

2. What did you do? _____

_____

Now read the paragraph.

EXAMPLE PARAGRAPH

Changing a Tire on Your Car

There are many steps in changing a tire on your car. Before you get started, make sure you have the following items: a <u>jack</u>, a <u>lug nut wrench</u>, and a <u>spare</u> tire. First, use the jack to <u>elevate</u> the car off the <u>ground</u>. This may require some <u>strength</u> because cars can be very heavy. Using the lug nut wrench, remove all of the lug nuts from the tire. This will probably be the most difficult step because some of the lug nuts may be "frozen." After you have taken off the lug nuts, remove the flat tire and replace it with your spare tire. <u>Screw</u> the lug nuts back onto the new tire, and check to see that they are <u>tightly</u> <u>fastened</u>. Finally, lower the car back down to the ground. Check one last time to make sure that the nuts are as tight as possible. Following these steps will have you back on the road <u>in no time</u>.

jack: tool that is used to raise a car to remove a tire

lug nut wrench: tool that is used to take the bolts off a car tire

spare: extra

elevate: raise

strength: power (the noun form of the adjective *strong*)

screw: twist

tightly: securely (opposite: loosely)

fastened: attached

in no time: very quickly

1. Put a check (✔) next to the statement that tells the purpose of the paragraph.

    _____ a. To tell the importance of a tire on a car

    _____ b. To show how to change the oil in a car

    _____ c. To tell why it is important to carry a spare tire

    _____ d. To show how to change a flat tire

2. Underline the topic sentence.

3. According to this paragraph, how many steps are there in changing a flat tire? _____

Five Features of a Good Topic Sentence

Good writers know that a topic sentence has the following features:

1. **guides the whole paragraph**	A well-written topic sentence controls or guides the whole paragraph. It lets the reader know what the rest of the paragraph will be about.
2. **not a well-known fact**	A good topic sentence is not a general fact that everyone accepts as true. For example, *Cars use gasoline* is not a good topic sentence because there is not much more to say about the topic.
3. **specific**	A good topic sentence is specific. *Minivans are useful* is not a good topic sentence because it is too general. The reader does not know exactly what to expect. *Minivans are useful to parents with three or more children* is a good topic sentence because it is specific. It gives a reason why minivans are useful and for whom.

4. not too specific   A good topic sentence is not too specific. *A Ford minivan can hold up to six adults* limits the topic. The supporting details have already been stated.

5. controlling idea   A good topic sentence has a controlling idea, a group of words or a phrase that helps to guide the flow if ideas in the paragraph: *A Toyota Corolla is the best car for a small family*. The underlined words are the controlling idea.

Activity 3   Recognizing Effective Topic Sentences

Consider what you already know about topic sentences. Then read each of the following groups of sentences. Write the general topic in the space provided. Put a check (✔) next to the best topic sentence.

1. General Topic: _digital cameras_

    _✔_ a. Digital cameras have more features than film cameras.

    _____ b. Digital cameras are expensive.

    _____ c. You can delete the pictures on a digital camera.

2. General topic: _____

    _____ a. Some cats are gray.

    _____ b. Cats are quiet, friendly, unique, beautiful, and smart.

    _____ c. Cats are easy to take care of.

3. General topic: _____

    _____ a. Pepperoni and mushrooms are my two favorite toppings on a pizza from Nino's.

    _____ b. Nino's pizzeria has a wide selection of delicious food.

    _____ c. Nino's makes good chicken-finger submarine sandwiches.

4. General topic: _____

     _____ a. Few people know the interesting history of snowboarding.

     _____ b. Snowboards are made of fiberglass and have sharp metal edges.

     _____ c. Snowboarding is a winter sport.

5. General topic: _____

     _____ a. My favorite seashell is the size of a football.

     _____ b. It is easiest to find seashells in the morning.

     _____ c. Seashells make great souvenirs.

Practice with Controlling Ideas

The controlling idea in your topic sentence guides the paragraph and lets the reader know what the paragraph is going to be about. The topic is limited by the controlling idea—it narrows the topic.

Here are some examples of topic sentences. The main subject is circled, and the controlling ideas are underlined.

1. (SUVs) are becoming more popular than compact cars.

   The reader expects to learn why SUVs are becoming popular.

2. (Electric staplers) are easier to use than other types of staplers.

   The reader expects to learn why electric staplers are so easy to use.

3. (Las Vegas) is a very popular vacation destination in the United States.

   The reader expects to learn why it is a popular vacation destination.

4. There are three things that people need to be aware of before (swimming in the ocean).

   The reader expects to learn about the three things, and this controlling idea in turn limits or narrows the topic.

Activity 4	Reviewing Topic Sentences and Controlling Ideas

Read each group of sentences. Put a check (✓) next to the best topic sentence. Underline the controlling idea in that sentence.

1. _____ a. Americans drink about 350 million cups of coffee every day.

   _____ b. Coffee is the drink of choice for many Americans.

   _____ c. Most Americans drink coffee in order to wake up in the morning.

2. _____ a. Yesterday was the tenth of April.

   _____ b. Yesterday I spilled spaghetti sauce on my shirt during my lunch break.

   _____ c. Yesterday I had a terrible day at work.

3. _____ a. My girlfriend and I had a wonderful time at Busch Gardens theme park yesterday.

   _____ b. We rode three different roller coasters.

   _____ c. My girlfriend and I enjoyed seeing the tigers and the monkeys.

4. _____ a. In the United States, 721,000 high school athletes participated in track and field last year.

   _____ b. The sport of track and field is very old.

   _____ c. The sport of track and field has increased in popularity in recent years.

5. _____ a. My iguana's trip to the vet's office was a catastrophe.

   _____ b. My iguana scratched the vet when she tried to pick it up.

   _____ c. People do not like iguanas.

| Activity 5 | Using Controlling Ideas to Limit or Narrow a Topic |

The following topic sentences are too general. Rewrite them and add controlling ideas.

1. Smoking is bad.

   _____

   _____

2. It is important to work hard.

   _____

   _____

3. The Smithsonian Institution's museums are located in Washington, D.C.

   _____

   _____

More Practice with Topic Sentences

| Activity 6 | Writing Topic Sentences |

Read each paragraph and write a topic sentence in the space provided. Be sure your sentence includes a controlling idea.

Paragraph 2 (cause-effect)

1. _____

   _____

   _____

It burns calories more quickly than any other form of exercise. In fact, running burns twice as many calories as swimming, the second best calorie-burning activity. While swimmers burn around 600 calories per hour, runners can burn up to 1200 calories per hour. Running is also a great form of exercise because it can be done almost anywhere. Finally, running is a budget-friendly activity; the only thing a runner needs to purchase is a good pair of running shoes.

Paragraph 3 (process)

2. _____

_____

_____

First, you can start by looking in the help wanted section of the newspaper. After checking the newspaper, you may want to look at online job sites, such as Monster.com or Jobs.com. After you find an interesting company, try visiting the company in person. Ask whether there are any openings even if no positions are advertised. Do not forget to have a good resume ready to give to a prospective employer. Make sure that it highlights all of your previous employment and education. Finally, remember that persistence is the key to getting the job you want. By following these steps, rest assured that you will find a job sooner rather than later.

Paragraph 4 (classification)

3. _____

_____

_____

Perhaps the best-known type of acting is television acting. This type of acting generally takes the form of television programs produced on studio lots. Another form of acting is stage acting. Plays are performed in many different <u>venues</u>: from large halls to small theaters. The third type of acting is film acting. Film acting begins with a screenplay, which includes all the written information about the set and the actors' dialogues, and grows into a movie. <u>Regardless of</u> the type of acting, it is safe to say that the spectators <u>appreciate</u> the <u>craft</u> of acting and the many hours of enjoyment it provides.

venues: places; locations

appreciate: recognize the value of; be glad about

regardless (of): no matter what; despite

craft: skill; expertise

Brainstorming

WRITER'S NOTE: Brainstorming

Imagine that you are on the fourth floor of a burning building. You need to think of some ways of escaping quickly. Can you think of at least three ways to escape? Discuss your answers as a group. Do not reject any ideas. Just write down as many different ideas as you can think of.

1. _____

2. _____

3. _____

Can you think of three ways to escape from a room on the fourth floor of a burning hotel?

Congratulations! You have just completed a brainstorming activity. **Brainstorming** is quickly writing down all the thoughts that come into your head. When you brainstorm, you do not think about whether the idea is good or bad or whether your writing is correct. You simply write to get your ideas on paper. The process is called brainstorming because it feels like there is a storm of ideas in your brain.

| **Activity 7** | **Brainstorming Practice** |

Choose one topic below to brainstorm in the space provided. Come up with at least four ideas. Then write a topic sentence for a paragraph about that topic. Be sure to include a controlling idea.

1. The best day of my life
2. How cell phones are changing our society
3. Why I like a particular type of movie
4. A place I would like to visit one day
5. Some dangers of going to the beach
6. A person who changed my life

Brainstorming Ideas

Topic sentence: _____

Activity 8	**Writing Your Own Paragraph**

Use your brainstorming notes and topic sentence from Activity 7 to write a paragraph below. Be sure that your topic sentence guides the whole paragraph.

_____

_____

_____

_____

_____

_____

_____

Supporting Detail Sentences

Think of **supporting detail sentences** as helpers for the topic sentence: They describe, explain, clarify, or give examples of the topic sentence. Supporting sentences support and explain the topic. They answer questions such as *Who? What? When? Where? Why?* and *How?* They explain the topic sentence in greater detail and give the reader more information.

Each paragraph that you write must have enough supporting details to make the main idea clear to the reader. Likewise, a good writer makes sure that each supporting sentence is related to the topic and its controlling ideas. Study the following examples.

1. Topic sentence: Many elderly people enjoy playing golf.

   Supporting sentence: Golf gives them an opportunity to exercise and socialize at the same time.

2. *Topic sentence:*   Emergency towing services are great to have in case your car breaks down.

   Supporting sentence: They can help you change a flat tire.

3. *Topic sentence:*   Cell phones allow parents to stay in better contact with their children.

   Supporting sentence: As long as his or her cell phone is turned on, a child can be reached at any time.

Types of Supporting Sentences

Good writers use many different kinds of supporting sentences. Good supporting sentences:

1. *Topic sentence:* There are many support services for students at the university.

   explain: These services, such as tutoring, are generally free for students.

2. *Topic sentence:* I will never forget my childhood home.

   describe: The house had a large entrance with a spiral staircase in the center.

3. *Topic sentence:* Note-taking is one of the most important study skills to learn.

   give reasons: Reviewing good notes before a test will help students become more familiar with the information.

4. *Topic sentence:* Jogging is not as easy as it appears.

   give facts: Ninety-seven percent of people cannot jog three miles without stopping.

5. *Topic sentence:* North Carolina has many natural resources.

   give examples: One type of emerald can be found in North Carolina.

Activity 9	Creating Questions Leading to Supporting Details

Read each topic sentence. What information would you expect the writer to include in the paragraph? For each topic sentence, write two questions that the supporting sentences should answer. Use Who? What? When? Where? Why? *or* How? *questions. The first one has been done for you.*

1. Pesticides should not be used on farm products.

   Why shouldn't pesticides be used on farm products? What do pesticides do to farm products? What kinds of pesticides?

2. The beaches along the Mediterranean Ocean are some of the best beaches in the world.

   _____

   _____

3. Although few people realize it, country music and rock music have some similar characteristics.

_____

_____

4. My boyfriend and I met in a very unlikely place.

_____

_____

Avoiding Unrelated Sentences

Some writers tend to give too much information about a topic. They try to include too many ideas in one paragraph. Remember that a paragraph should focus on just one controlling idea at a time. Every sentence must support the topic sentence in some way. These supporting sentences help maintain the unity of the paragraph. (For more practice on unity, see Unit 2, pages 28–49.) The following activity will help you to identify good supporting sentences.

Activity 10   **Identifying Good Supporting Sentences**

Read each paragraph. For each numbered sentence, write "good supporting sentence" or "unrelated sentence" below. Then explain your answer.

Paragraph 5 (classification)

EXAMPLE PARAGRAPH

The Features of a Good Restaurant

There are certain qualities that make for a good restaurant. Good restaurants provide fast and friendly service. The hostess and server are friendly and courteous at all times. In addition, the server makes sure that customers receive their food in a timely fashion. (1) Since customers go to a restaurant to eat, obviously the quality of the food is important. (2) Some of the best-quality cheeses can be imported from France. A good restaurant also uses fresh ingredients in its dishes, which are usually served hot. (3) Good restaurants also have a good atmosphere. They pay attention to details such as the decorations, the lighting, and the cleanliness.

1. _____   _____

_____

_____

2. _____   _____

_____

_____

3. _____   _____

_____

_____

Paragraph 6 (descriptive)

A Capital Trip

One of my greatest vacations was spent in Washington, D.C. (1) The first thing I did on my arrival was to visit some of the Smithsonian Institution's museums. These museums were gigantic, with elaborate marble floors and pillars that reached dizzying heights. I spent three days visiting these museums, which are free to the public, and then I saw some impressive memorials. The Lincoln Memorial was immense. After reading the Gettysburg Address at the Lincoln Memorial, I decided to walk down the mall to the Vietnam Memorial. I was moved by the tranquility and simplicity of the long, black wall dedicated to all the soldiers who were killed during this war. (2) My final day in Washington was spent just walking around. Because it was April, I even got to see the famous cherry blossoms in bloom. (3) Although April is a spring month, some types of trees do not bloom until late summer. Clearly, the museums in Washington, D.C., make for a great trip.

1. _____   _____

_____

_____

_____

2. _____   _____

_____

_____

_____

3. _____   _____

_____

_____

_____

LANGUAGE FOCUS 1: Identifying Verbs and Fragments

Every sentence in English has a verb. Look at the underlined verbs in these examples.

For years, Houstonians <u>have complained</u> about the traffic problem in their city.

Contrary to the opinion of some tourists, American cuisine <u>is</u> a rich mixture of many different sources and traditions.

Through the careful study of geography, teachers <u>can</u> at the same time <u>help</u> their <u>students</u> with history.

Read aloud the same three sentences without the verbs. A sentence without a verb is called a fragment. A fragment is a serious error in composition. You will practice fragments in this unit and others in this book.

Activity 11   **Checking for Fragments**

Read these sentences about a way to study vocabulary. The subject in each clause is underlined. Circle the verb that goes with each subject. If all subjects have a verb, then write CORRECT on the line. If a verb is missing, write FRAGMENT on the line and add an appropriate verb in the correct place. The first two have been done for you.

___correct___ , ___fragment___   1. <u>Students</u> (come across) an incredible amount of new vocabulary every day as <u>they</u> English.
                                             read

_____   2. Some <u>learners</u> this problem by using flashcards.

_____ , _____   3. What are <u>flashcards</u>, and how do <u>you</u> use them?

_____   4. A <u>flashcard</u> a small card for learning vocabulary.

_____ , _____   5. <u>Learners</u> write the new word on one side of the card, and <u>they</u> a definition on the other side.

_____   6. Serious <u>learners</u> flashcards every day or two to learn new vocabulary.

LANGUAGE FOCUS 2: Nouns and Noun Forms

There are two kinds of nouns: count and noncount. If you can count a noun (five sandwiches, nine ideas), then there is a singular form (sandwich, idea) and a plural form (sandwiches, ideas). If you cannot count a noun (pollution, art, hair), there is only one form.

In writing, pay attention to adjectives that are used with plural nouns. Here are some examples:

these methods   several people   numerous cases

two tests   many reasons   other decisions

A common error is to forget to use the plural form of the noun. Study this example with three errors:

Many **scientist** attended the recent meeting in Seattle. At that meeting, there were many **presentation** about the numerous **effect** of global warming.

Activity 12   **Editing for Noun Forms**

Read these sentences about people who take care of their elders. Look at the nouns that are boxed. If there is an error in noun form, make a correction above the word. The first one has been done for you.

1. More than twenty-two million ~~family~~ *families* face the daily challenges of taking care of their elders.

2. It is only logical that this number will grow in the rest of this centuries as our population soars.

3. Most of the people who take care of their parents or other family member work at a regular job all day.

4. About forty percent of those who care for their elder also take care of their own children.

5. Over seventy percent of caregivers are women, and nearly one third of these women are over the age of 65.

6. An amazing eight of ten of these caregiver provide care for an average of four hour a day, seven days a week.

Connecting Topic Sentences and Supporting Details

| Activity 13 | Brainstorming for Topic Sentences |

For each topic, brainstorm ideas for topic sentences. (You will use your topic sentences to practice supporting ideas in Activity 14.)

1. Your favorite animal

Topic sentence: _____

2. A person you know

Topic sentence: _____

3. A city

Topic sentence: _____

Activity 14   **Asking the Right Questions**

Choose one of the topic sentences you created in Activity 13. Write questions for it using the interrogative words. If you cannot think of at least three questions, perhaps your topic sentence is weak. For more practice, repeat this activity with other topic sentences.

1. Topic sentence: <u>One of the worst airline disasters in modern times occurred three decades ago.</u>

   Who?   <u>Who was involved in the disaster?</u>

   What?   <u>What happened?</u>

   When?   <u>When did this happen?</u>

   Where?   <u>Where did the disaster happen?</u>

   Why?   <u>Why did the disaster happen?</u>

   Other: <u>How many people died in the disaster?</u>

2. Topic sentence: _____

   _____

   Who?   _____

   What?   _____

   When?   _____

   Where?   _____

   Why?   _____

   Other: _____

Activity 15   **Writing Supporting Sentences**

Look at your topic sentence and questions from Activity 14. Write supporting sentences that answer each question you created.

Topic sentence: _____

_____

1. _____

_____

_____

2. _____

_____

_____

3. _____

_____

_____

4. _____

_____

_____

5. _____

_____

_____

6. _____

_____

_____

Activity 16 — **Writing a Paragraph**

Use the supporting sentences and the topic sentence from Activity 15 to write a paragraph. Be sure to use only supporting sentences that relate to the topic sentence and its controlling idea.

_____

_____

_____

_____

_____

_____

_____

_____

_____

_____

_____

Concluding Sentences

A **concluding sentence** concludes, or wraps up, a paragraph. It lets the reader know that you are finished talking about the idea introduced by the topic sentence.

Features of a Concluding Sentence

A concluding sentence has two main features:

1. It is usually the last sentence of a paragraph.

2. It lets the reader know that the paragraph has ended.

A concluding sentence can:

1. **restate**   It restates the main idea of the topic sentence.

   (Paragraph 6, "A Capital Trip") Clearly, the museums in Washington, D.C., make for a great trip.

2. **reach a logical conclusion**   It lets the reader know that the paragraph has come
                                            to a logical conclusion by offering a suggestion,
                                            giving an opinion, or making a prediction.

   (Paragraph 1, "Changing the Tire on Your Car") Following these steps will have you back on the

   road in no time. (prediction)

Transitions with Concluding Sentences

> Here is a list of transitional words and phrases that are commonly used at the beginning of concluding sentences. Try to use these in the activities that follow.
>
> | | | |
> |---|---|---|
> | because of this | indeed | hence |
> | as a result | overall | for this reason |
> | certainly | in the end | surely |
> | in conclusion | therefore | for these reasons |
> | clearly | thus | in sum |
>
> **In conclusion**, successful businesses are the result of the actions of good workers.
>
> **Clearly**, buying a used car has more advantages than buying a brand-new car.

NOTE: You will find transition boxes placed strategically throughout this text to help you learn where you can add transitional words.

| Activity 17 | **Writing Concluding Sentences** |

Go back to Paragraph 2 (p. 9) and Paragraph 5 (p. 14). Write a concluding sentence for each. Label the type that you used. Use a different type of concluding statement for each paragraph.

1. Paragraph 2 (p. 9) (about exercise):

   _____

   _____

   _____

2. Paragraph 5 (p. 14) (about restaurants):

   _____

   _____

   _____

REVIEW: FOUR FEATURES OF A WELL-WRITTEN PARAGRAPH

All good paragraphs have four key features in common.

1. **main idea**	**A paragraph has a topic sentence that states the main idea.** The topic sentence is like a short summary of the paragraph. It lets the reader know what the paragraph will be about. It contains the main subject and a controlling idea.
2. **one topic**	**All of the sentences are about one topic.** Each sentence of the paragraph relates to the topic sentence and its controlling idea. This helps to maintain the *coherence* of the paragraph. (You will learn about this in the next unit.)
3. **indented**	**The first sentence of a paragraph is indented.** Remember that the first line of a paragraph starts about a half inch in from the margin. You do this on a word processor by pressing the "tab" key.

4. good concluding sentence

The last sentence, or concluding sentence, brings the paragraph to a logical conclusion. Sometimes the concluding sentence is a restatement of the topic sentence. At other times, writers offer suggestions, opinions, or predictions based on the writer's purpose.

| Activity 18 | Analyzing the Features of a Paragraph |

Read the paragraph and answer the questions that follow.

Paragraph 7 (opinion)

EXAMPLE PARAGRAPH

The Dark Side of Cycling

Because illegal drug use has plagued the world of professional cycling for decades, it must be stopped. Certain drugs help cyclists ride faster and farther than normal. Some of the drugs work by increasing the number of red blood cells in the body. While the drugs might help the athletes to perform better, there can be terrible side effects. In the year and a half before the 2004 Tour de France, nine professional cyclists died from overdoses of illegal drugs. Many professional baseball players are also involved in a drug controversy. Despite the danger, more and more cyclists are turning to these drugs to gain an advantage over their competition. It is unfortunate that these athletes value their races more than their lives.

1. What is the topic? _____

   _____

2. What is the topic sentence? _____

   _____

3. What is the concluding sentence? _____

   _____

4. Is the concluding sentence a restatement, a suggestion, an opinion, or a prediction? _____

5. Which sentence does not belong? _____

   _____

6. Explain why the sentence you have chosen does not belong. _____

_____

7. What is the writer's main purpose for writing this paragraph? _____

_____

8. Can you suggest any ways to improve this paragraph? _____

_____

Activity 19   Bringing It All Together

Read each paragraph and underline the topic sentence. Then circle the sentence that is not a good supporting sentence (you will find one per paragraph). Write a concluding sentence on the lines that follow. If possible, use transitions from the box on page 22.

Paragraph 8 (definition)

EXAMPLE PARAGRAPH

Writing Centers

Writing centers are wonderful places on college campuses where students can go to get help with their writing. Writing center tutors generally do not proofread a student's paper but rather find repeated mistakes in the paper and teach the student how to avoid making those mistakes in the future. Writing centers can help students in areas such as grammar, punctuation, brainstorming, organization, and format. Typically, more women use writing centers than men. Many students also go to writing centers to get help in doing research or documenting outside sources. The help that students receive at writing centers is valuable as many centers are staffed by English professors or professional writers.

Concluding sentence: _____

_____

_____

Paragraph 9 (cause-effect)

EXAMPLE PARAGRAPH

Body Art

Young adults choose to get tattoos for a number of reasons. Some carefully select a design for its artistic value. They may even create the design themselves. Some get tattoos to make a rebellious statement. Political views or expressions against the status quo are common examples of tattoos, especially on young people. Many people like to get tattoos done on their lower back. Some tattoos have a special meaning for the owner. They may represent a variety of things from a lover to a deceased relative. Some people get tattoos in order to look better. For instance, some use tattoo art to cover up scars or as a way to get permanent makeup.

Concluding sentence: _____

_____

_____

Activity 20   **Writing Your Own Paragraph**

Choose one of the topic sentences from Activity 1, page 3, and develop it into a paragraph. Be sure to

- *indent*

- *start with a topic sentence*

- *make sure the topic sentence has a controlling idea*

- *add supporting sentences that relate to the controlling idea in the topic sentence*

- *end with a concluding sentence*

Be sure to include the four features of a well-written paragraph from pages 23 and 24.

Your topic: _____

Brainstorming Ideas

Title _____

_____

_____

_____

_____

_____

_____

_____

_____

Activity 21   **Peer Editing**

Exchange with a classmate the paragraph you wrote in Activity 20. Use Peer Editing Sheet 1 on page 161. Be sure to offer positive suggestions and comments that will help the writer write a better paragraph. Consider your classmate's comments as you revise your paragraph.

Tips for Peer Editing

- Begin by saying something positive about the paper. Be nice.

- Answer the questions completely on the Peer Editing Sheet. Be specific.

- Find a straightforward but polite way to suggest improvements. Make suggestions in a direct but constructive way. Avoid statements such as "This is very bad" or "You don't make any sense." Instead, use statements such as "I found this part a bit confusing because . . ." or "What do you mean to say here?"

- When you return the Peer Editing Sheet, invite discussion with the writer about the essay.

 **Online Study Center**   For more practice, go to the *Great Paragraphs to Great Essays* website at http://esl.college.hmco.com/students

Five Elements of Good Writing

Writing Goal:	Understanding purpose, audience, clarity, unity, coherence
Language Focus 3:	Using clear, descriptive language
Language Focus 4:	Clear pronoun reference
Examples:	Paragraphs 10–14

WHAT MAKES A GOOD PARAGRAPH?

Now you know the basic parts of a paragraph:

topic sentence

controlling idea

supporting sentences

concluding sentence

transition

It is extremely important for you to understand these key concepts, but there is more to good writing than just knowing the parts of a paragraph.

The next step to improving your writing is to move beyond words and sentences. You must learn to consider how all of the sentences interact with each other and with the reader. In this unit, you will learn five elements of good writing:

- purpose
- unity
- audience
- coherence
- clarity

FIVE ELEMENTS OF GOOD WRITING

Element 1: Purpose

When we talk about the **purpose** of a paragraph, we are talking about the reasons that a writer is writing a paragraph. For writers to stay focused on the topic, they must understand the purpose that they are trying to accomplish. The purpose is the goal the writer is trying to achieve.

The three most common purposes of academic writing are

- to inform

- to persuade

- to entertain

If you think about it, anything you have ever written has served one or more of these three purposes.

Activity 1   Analyzing a Paragraph

Answer the questions on the basis of your experiences. Then read the paragraph and answer the questions below it.

1. Have you ever used a grill? For what occasion? Where?

   _____

   _____

   _____

2. Why do some people choose to grill food rather than cook it in the kitchen?

   _____

   _____

   _____

Paragraph 10 (process)

EXAMPLE PARAGRAPH

Grilling

Preparing a grill for a summer cookout is easy if you follow certain steps. First, it is important to start with a clean grill, so you should remove all <u>rust</u> from the grilling surface. After removing the top <u>rack</u>, place one layer of <u>briquettes</u> in the bottom rack. <u>Stack</u> the briquettes in a pyramid shape with the highest point at the center of the grill. Once the briquettes have been stacked, cover them with lighter fluid. Make sure the liquid is not near any open <u>flame</u> as you cover the <u>charcoal</u>. After the charcoal has been <u>soaked</u> in fluid, use a long match or a long lighter to ignite it. Be careful not to burn yourself since the <u>fumes</u> of the lighter fluid may ignite before the charcoal catches fire. Next, wait for the flames to die out and the charcoal to turn white. Finally, spread the briquettes out in an even layer and replace the top rack. Once you have followed these simple steps, you are ready to grill!

rust: corroded metal

rack: metal grid on which food is cooked

briquettes: fuel used for grilling

stack: to pile on top of

flame: fire

charcoal: same as briquette

soaked: very wet

fumes: vapors, odors, or exhaust

3. What is the writer's purpose in writing this paragraph?

_____

_____

_____

4. Does the writer stay focused on one idea or topic? If not, explain where the writer gets off topic.

_____

_____

5. Do you think the writer achieved his or her goal in writing this paragraph? Explain.

_____

_____

Purpose Statement

Good writers often remind themselves of their writing topics as they write. Here is a tool to help you maintain the focus of your paragraph. Writers often create a **purpose statement** before they begin.

A purpose statement is a short sentence that clearly defines the purpose of the paragraph, which is the reason that you are writing this information. The purpose statement will help you to stay within your topic and maintain the focus of your writing. You can think of a purpose statement as a type of pre–topic sentence exercise.

Purpose statements are simple and to the point. For example, if you are going to write a paragraph about how to clean your room, your purpose statement would read something like this:

The purpose of this paragraph is to **explain how to clean your room**.

Although this might seem obvious, many writers fail to remain "on topic." That is, some writers lose focus and begin to write about other information. It can be very easy to include material that does not fit in the paragraph. This extra information might belong in a new paragraph, or you might not need it at all. If you use a purpose statement, you can check that each sentence in the paragraph does indeed fulfill the purpose of that paragraph.

Here are some sample topics followed by example purpose statements:

Topic:	How to play "fish"
Purpose Statement:	The purpose of this paragraph is to explain to the reader how to play the card game called "fish."
Topic:	The effects of insufficient sleep
Purpose Statement:	The purpose of this paragraph is to tell the negative effects or results of not getting enough sleep each day.
Topic:	The messiest room that I have ever seen
Purpose Statement:	The purpose of this paragraph is to describe the messiest room that I have ever seen.

Activity 2   **Writing Purpose Statements**

Read each of the following topics. Then write a purpose statement for each. The first one has been done for you.

1. *Topic:* your craziest experience in a restaurant

   Purpose statement: The purpose of this paragraph is to tell about the time that my uncle

   started a food fight in McDonald's.

2. *Topic:* Alternative sources of energy

   Purpose statement: _____

   _____

3. Topic: The most important invention of the last century

   Purpose statement: _____

   _____

4. Topic: My worst family vacation

   Purpose statement: _____

   _____

5. Topic: The effects of smoking

   Purpose statement: _____

   _____

6. Topic: How to learn up to fifty idioms per day

   Purpose statement: _____

   _____

Element 2: Audience

The second element of good writing is **audience**. The term *audience* refers to the readers that the writer expects to read the paragraph. Good writers know who their audience is before they start writing.

Techniques for Establishing Audience

Consider these two main techniques for establishing audience:

- person (**first**, **second**, or **third**)
- formal or informal

Person

Writers can choose among three different **persons**, or points of view, when writing.
The **first person** refers to the person or thing that is speaking. Paragraphs written in the first person use first-person pronouns (*I*, *we*) or first-person possessive adjectives (*my* and *our*). Paragraphs that explain personal experiences often use the first person.

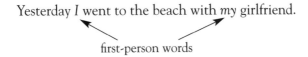

Yesterday *I* went to the beach with *my* girlfriend.

first-person words

The **second person** refers to the person or thing that is being spoken to. It is usually used to give directions or instructions. The second person is often used for informal writing. Paragraphs written in the second person use second-person pronouns (*you* and *yours*) and the second-person possessive adjective (*your*). Process paragraphs often use the second person (with or without the pronoun *you*.)

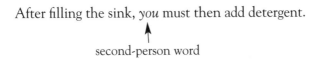

After filling the sink, *you* must then add detergent.

second-person word

The **third person** refers to the person or thing that is being spoken about. Think of the third person as someone telling a story about another person or thing. Paragraphs written in the third person use third-person pronouns (*he, she, it, they, him, her, them, his, hers, theirs*) and third-person possessive adjectives (*his, her, their*). Most academic paragraphs use third person.

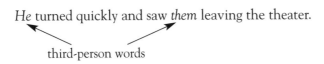

He turned quickly and saw *them* leaving the theater.

third-person words

A paragraph should stay consistent with respect to person. In other words, good writers do not shift between first, second, and third person within one piece of writing.

Activity 3	**Recognizing Person**

The following sentences change person within the sentence (unnecessary shifts in person). Rewrite the sentences, changing the incorrect pronoun. (Hint: Pay careful attention to the pronouns in the sentences.)

1. When a person goes shopping, you should always look for sales.

   _____

   _____

2. One should carpool if you want to save on gas.

   _____

   _____

3. Doctors warn people that you should watch what you eat.

   _____

   _____

4. Jeff brought pizza home for dinner. He told his mother that you should wait until it cooled down before eating it.

   _____

   _____

Choosing Person in Formal or Informal Writing

Most of the writing that you do for school is considered formal writing. The first person is generally used in writing a personal story or description. In most cases, academic writing uses formal techniques in the third person. If you are unsure about the formality level of an assignment, ask your instructor for more details.

Discuss these questions with a partner or a small group:

1. When do you think you would use informal writing?

2. What person do you think you should use for formal writing?

3. What person do you think you should use for informal writing?

Certain topics work better using a particular person (first, second, or third). Here are some examples of topics, the person you can use for each, and the level of writing.

Topic	Person	Level of Writing
1. The importance of voting	Third	Formal
2. A letter to your best friend	First or second	Informal
3. Description of your best vacation	First	Formal or informal, depending on audience

Activity 4   Identifying Audience

Read each topic and decide whether it requires first, second, or third person. Then decide whether the writing should be formal or informal. There may be more than one correct answer. The first one has been done for you.

Topic	Person	Formal or Informal
1. A letter to your cousin	First and second person	informal
2. A paragraph about the causes of the Civil War	_____	_____
3. A paragraph about your trip to Mexico	_____	_____
4. A paragraph telling how to bake a cake	_____	_____
5. A paragraph telling why you would make a good president	_____	_____

Element 3: Clarity

Clarity refers to how easy it is for the reader to understand your writing. Good writers explain their point easily and clearly. Clear sentences are not vague or indirect; they get the point across to the reader by using specific, concise language. The two Language Focus reviews in this chapter can help writers to achieve better clarity.

Features: Here are two ways that you can improve clarity:

- use **descriptive (or precise) words**

- use **clear pronoun references**

LANGUAGE FOCUS 3: Using Clear, Descriptive Language

To improve clarity, it is important for writers to choose words that give an accurate description of their topic. Some words are vague and unclear, and good writers avoid them. You can think of these unclear words as being too common or boring. An example of one of these words is *nice*. Read the following sentence:

> Although there were far more Republican voters than Democrats in the presidential election of 1976, people voted for the Democratic candidate because they perceived him as being nice.

The adjective *nice* does not tell us very much about the candidate. It does very little to tell us why voters chose this candidate over any other. An effective writer would choose a more descriptive word to inform readers.

> Although there were far more Republican voters than Democrats in the presidential election of 1976, people voted for the Democratic candidate because they perceived him as being sincere.

In this sentence, the word *sincere* is more descriptive and informative than the word *nice*. For a sentence to express the exact meaning that the writer wants to share with readers, the writer must use clear and precise words.

Activity 5 — Choosing Clear and Precise Words

Replace each of the unclear or boring words with three more descriptive or precise words. The first two have been done for you.

1. good   wonderful   great   delightful

2. bad   horrible   terrible   awful

3. fun   _____   _____   _____

4. big   _____   _____   _____

5. small   _____   _____   _____

6. old   _____   _____   _____

WRITER'S NOTE: Adding Description

Good writers also strive to make their writing clear and specific by adding adjectives or prepositional phrases.

Original:	The soldiers slowly crossed the river.
More specific:	The soldiers slowly crossed the dangerous river.
	The soldiers slowly crossed the river in the dark.
	The soldiers slowly crossed the dangerous river in the dark.
	The tired soldiers slowly crossed the dangerous river in the dark.

Adding adjectives or prepositional phrases can make your sentences more specific and descriptive to improve the clarity of your writing.

Activity 6   **Choosing Descriptive Phrases**

Replace each unclear or simple phrase with a more descriptive or accurate phrase.

the old house _____   in the dark house _____

the long road _____   the wide street _____

a nice gift _____   the good dessert _____

Clarity in Sentences

Just as it is important to maintain clarity at the word level, it is also important at the sentence level. The following unclear sentences are followed by revised versions.

Vague or unclear	**Clear**
1. The guy went to the store.	Miguel went to the hardware store to purchase a power drill.
2. Jennifer took her things with her when she went out.	Jennifer took her sunblock, a radio, and a towel to the beach.
3. The house was dark.	The house was dimly lit; the only source of light came from a candle in the hallway.

Activity 7 — Rewriting for Clarity and Description

Rewrite each vague sentence and improve its clarity with more descriptive words. Make sure your new sentence has the same meaning as the original sentence.

1. That person knows a lot about computers.

   Rewrite: _____

   _____

2. His clothes looked nice.

   Rewrite: _____

   _____

3. The store is big.

   Rewrite: _____

   _____

4. After eating, we went to a house.

   Rewrite: _____

   _____

Activity 8 — Analyzing a Paragraph

Answer the questions based on your experiences. Then read the paragraph and answer the questions below it.

1. Have you ever noticed the workers in a restaurant? What types of jobs do the employees of a restaurant do?

   _____

   _____

2. What do you think it is like to work in a restaurant's kitchen?

_____

_____

Paragraph 11 (description)

Behind the Scenes in a Restaurant

EXAMPLE PARAGRAPH

A restaurant kitchen can be a very <u>hectic</u> place. Chefs shout at the staff while they are busy preparing and cooking the food. <u>Servers</u> <u>hustle</u> in and out of the kitchen at a <u>tremendous</u> <u>pace</u> to hurry the food to the hungry customers. When the customers finish eating, <u>bussers</u> rush the empty plates back into the kitchen and carelessly drop them into the huge sinks. Maintaining this constant flow of traffic in the kitchen is a complicated <u>juggling</u> act. The action in a restaurant kitchen never stops.

hectic: busy
servers: waiters or waitresses
hustle: hurry; move quickly
tremendous: very big

pace: speed
bussers: helpers in a restaurant who
   clean tables
juggling: balancing

3. Draw a box around the topic sentence. Circle the main subject and underline the controlling idea.

4. What is the main purpose of this paragraph? In other words, what is the writer's intent in writing this essay?

_____

_____

5. Underline the concluding sentence.

6. What type of concluding sentence is it? (circle one)

   restatement / suggestion / opinion / prediction

Activity 9   Clarity in a Paragraph

Refer to paragraph 11 to answer the questions below about clarity.

1. Write four words that name specific people.

   _____

2. How do these words add to the clarity of the writer's message?

   _____

3. Write one of the phrases that means to do something quickly. _____

4. Skilled writers try to use specific adjectives to help readers understand the setting as much as possible. Write the adjectives that precede the nouns below.

   _____ place   _____ sinks

   _____ pace   _____ flow

   _____ plates   _____ juggling act

Language Focus 4: Clear Pronoun Reference

Another thing that good writers do to maintain clarity is to make sure that every pronoun refers to a specific noun. If the exact meaning, or reference, of the pronoun is not clear, then repeat the noun or use a synonym of that noun.

> Children should not be allowed to watch R-rated movies for many reasons. <u>They</u> say that these movies can disturb the children.

In the above sentence, who is "they"? Does *they* refer to the children? To R-rated movies? To people in general? Because we do not know who or what *they* refers to, this is considered an unclear pronoun reference. The easiest way to correct it is to use the precise noun. In this case, it would be better to say

> Children should not be allowed to watch R-rated movies for many reasons. <u>Most psychologists</u> say that these movies can disturb the children.

| Activity 10 | Editing for Clear Pronoun References |

Read the following sentences about food. The number in parentheses is the number of pronouns in the sentence. Circle every pronoun. If there is a reference, and if the reference is not clear, change the pronoun to make the meaning of the sentence clear. The first one has been done for you.

1. My favorite desserts are chocolate cream pie and carrot cake. (I) like (it) so much because of the creamy texture and of course the incredible chocolate flavor. (2)

    Change "it" to chocolate cream pie.

2. Chili is a kind of thick soup made with ground meat. Some people prepare it with beans. They like the combination of tastes. (2)

    _____

3. My uncle cooked chicken, corn, and potatoes for dinner. My cousin Frank liked them, but he did not like the corn. (2)

    _____

4. One of the easiest dishes to prepare is hummus. Hummus is a very thick dip made from mashed garbanzo beans. They are then mixed with tahini paste. It tastes great. (2)

    _____

| Activity 11 | **Editing for Clear Pronoun References** |

The following paragraph contains six errors with pronoun reference. Improve the clarity of the sentences by changing the boxed words to words or phrases that are more specific.

Paragraph 12 (compare/contrast)

EXAMPLE PARAGRAPH

The Weather in Chicago and Miami

My cousin and I recently had a discussion about whether his hometown, Chicago, or my hometown, Miami, has better weather. Our discussion centered on three differences between the weather in our two hometowns. First, Chicago has all four seasons, but Miami does not. Chicago enjoys summer, fall, winter, and spring weather. (1) It, in contrast, has only two seasons: a very mild winter and a very long summer. Another major difference in the weather between our two cities is that (2) its worst weather occurs in the winter. On the average, the high temperature reaches only around 32 degrees, and the low each night goes down to about 20 degrees. Unlike in Chicago, the problem in (3) it is not the cold but rather the heat. In the summer, the daytime temperature reaches 95 degrees and drops to only 75 or so at night. Finally, (4) they worry about different weather problems. While a Chicagoan's biggest weather fear is a blizzard, the biggest weather problem for (5) them is a hurricane. In the end, (6) we learned that each of our hometowns has unique weather.

Vague word	**Better clarity**
1. it	_____
2. its	_____
3. it	_____
4. they	_____
5. them	_____
6. we	_____

Element 4: Unity

Unity in a paragraph means that all the sentences are related to the topic sentence and its controlling idea. Good writers stay on topic by making sure that each supporting detail sentence relates to the topic sentence.

Activity 12   Analyzing Unity

Read the following paragraph. Underline the sentence that does not belong.

Paragraph 13 (process)

EXAMPLE PARAGRAPH

Cleaning 101

(1) Cleaning your room is not difficult if you follow some simple <u>guidelines</u>. (2) First, you must you must pick up all of your clothes off the floor. (3) Then you need to decide which clothes are dirty and which clothes are clean and put them in their appropriate places. (4) It is important to wash your clothes with good-quality laundry detergent to keep them looking neat and clean. (5) After that, you should put away any items that are out of place. (6) The next step is to <u>dust</u> all of your furniture, such as your <u>nightstand</u> or your <u>dresser</u>. (7) The final step is to <u>mop</u> or <u>vacuum</u> the floor, depending on the surface. (8) When you have finished these steps, you can relax as you think about your good work.

guidelines: general rules to follow
dust: to clean with a dry cloth
nightstand: small table next to a bed
dresser: furniture used to contain clothing

mop: to clean a floor with soap and water
vacuum: to clean a floor with a type of machine

You can use a purpose statement to help establish your purpose, and you can also use it to help establish unity. You can also check to see whether each sentence follows the writer's purpose statement: "The purpose of this paragraph is to explain how to clean your room." Study these questions and answers about Paragraph 13.

1. Does the first sentence maintain the unity of the paragraph?

   Yes. Here, the first sentence is the topic sentence. It lets readers know that

   the paragraph will give the steps necessary to clean their room.

2. Does the second sentence maintain the unity of the paragraph?

   Yes. It gives the first step to cleaning your room.

3. Does the third sentence maintain the unity of the paragraph?

   Yes. It provides information describing what to do with the clothes. It provides

   extra information about the second sentence.

4. Does the fourth sentence maintain the unity of the paragraph?

   No. It tells the reader about the importance of doing laundry with a specific type of laundry

   detergent. Because sentence 4 does not support the purpose of the paragraph, it should

   not be included.

5. Do sentences 5–7 maintain the unity of the paragraph?

   Yes, each gives a step in how to clean your room.

6. What about sentence 8? Does it belong?

   Yes. This is the concluding sentence for the ideas in this paragraph. It sums up everything.

Activity 13   Maintaining Unity

Read the following paragraph. Two of the sentences do not belong. Write the numbers of these two sentences and be prepared to explain why the sentences do not belong.

Paragraph 14 (classification)

EXAMPLE PARAGRAPH

The Many Faces of Acting

   (1) Modern acting comes in a variety of forms and can be classified in three ways: television acting, stage acting, and film acting. (2) Perhaps the best-known type of acting is television acting. (3) This type of acting generally takes the form of television programs produced on studio lots. (4) Many actors started their careers as waiters or waitresses in Hollywood. (5) Another form of acting is stage acting. (6) In stage acting, the same performance is repeated, and the sets stay the same for each performance. (7) The shows are performed in places from large halls to small theaters. (8) Plays that are performed on stage can be very enjoyable. (9) Finally, there is film acting. (10) Film acting begins with a screenplay, which includes all the written information about the set and the actors' dialogues, and grows into a movie. (11) Whichever form it takes—television, stage, or film—acting is a form of entertainment that many people enjoy.

1. Sentence number: _____

_____

_____

2. Sentence number: _____

_____

_____

Element 5: Coherence

A piece of writing is said to have coherence when all of its parts are organized and flow smoothly and logically from one idea to the next. Writers strive for coherence so that the reader can follow along more easily.

Features: Three important features of coherence are

- logical order

- repetition of key words

- use of transitional words and phrases

Logical Order

It is important to follow a logical order in your writing. The next activity will help you to understand the importance of logical order.

Activity 14   Sequencing Information

The following sentences form a paragraph, but they are not in the best order. Read the sentences and then number them from one to five to indicate the best order.

a. _____ He starts his day by putting on face makeup and a large red nose.

b. _____ When he arrives, he puts on a performance that includes jokes, balloon animals, funny stories, and magic tricks.

c. _____ When his performance ends and the audience is happy, Michael returns home, satisfied that he has done his job as a clown well.

d. _____ Michael's typical day at work is far from ordinary.

e. _____ He then puts on his oversize shoes and gets into his polka-dotted car and drives to a different location each day, usually a birthday party or other special event.

Repetition of Key Words

Good writers know that certain key words need to be repeated in a paragraph to keep the reader focused on the topic. Sometimes students worry that using the same word again and again can sound too repetitive. To avoid this, writers can also use pronouns to take the place of these key nouns. For example, look at the paragraph that you put in order in Activity 14 and answer the following questions:

1. What is the main subject of the paragraph?

   _____

2. What is the writer's purpose?

   _____

3. What key words (nouns or pronouns) does the writer repeat to keep the reader focused on the topic?

   _____

Transitional Words and Phrases

Transitional words and phrases are essential to maintain the flow and coherence of a paragraph. They are the links between ideas.

Commonly Used Transition Words and Phrases			
To give examples:	*for example* *for instance*		
To add information:	*and* *next* *in addition* *first*		
To compare or contrast:	*in contrast* *by comparison* *on the other hand*		
To show time:	*finally* *after* *before* *when*		
To emphasize:	*for these reasons* *obviously* *without a doubt*		
To show sequence:	*first (second, third, etc.)* *next* *at the same time*		
To summarize:	*therefore* *thus* *in conclusion*		

PROOFREADING

WRITER'S NOTE: Proofread Your Work

Good writers know that it takes more than just one session of writing to create a good paragraph. Proofreading is an essential last step in the revision process. Try to proofread your work at least twice before turning it in to your teacher.

Five Proofreading Strategies

Proofreading sounds like an easy thing to do, but many writers have trouble doing a good job proofreading their work. You will be much happier with your final writing assignment if you follow these suggestions.

1. **Take a break from the work.** Give yourself time after you have finished writing. The more time you take the better. A day or more is ideal, but even a break of five or ten minutes helps.

2. **Read your writing aloud.** Reading your work aloud, even if you are just mumbling it to yourself, does two things. It helps you to read your work more carefully and slowly, and it helps you to catch more errors.

3. **Read your paper backward.** Start proofreading your writing with the last sentence. Then read the second to last sentence, the third to last, and so on. This technique can help you to find more grammatical errors.

4. **Cover your work.** With another piece of paper, cover up everything except the line that you are reading. This will help you to focus more closely on each line.

5. **Pretend that you are someone else.** Read your paper as a reader, not as a writer. Reading your work through the eyes of the reader will help you to identify phrases or sentences that might be unclear. One way to do this effectively is to read your paper after you have taken a break from it for two or three days (or longer). You will be amazed at how many words, ideas, and sentences you will want to change.

WRITER'S NOTE: Titles for Your Work

A paragraph can have a title, but it is not necessary. An essay, on the other hand, always has a title.

The title of a work should be short. It should not be a complete sentence. Your title should describe the contents of the whole work. All important words (including the first word) should be capitalized.

Study the titles of the paragraphs in Units 1, 2, and 3 to learn about effective titles.

Activity 15	Writing Your Own Paragraph

Choose one of the topic sentences that you wrote in Activity 13, page 18, in Unit 1 and develop it into a paragraph. (Do not choose the sentence that you already developed into a paragraph in Unit 1, Activity 16, page 21.)

Your topic: _____

Brainstorming Box

Purpose statement: _____

_____

As you write, be sure to

- include the four features of a well-written paragraph from page 23 in Unit 1

- consider your audience and person (first, second, third)

- depending on your topic and your audience, decide whether to write in a formal or informal style

- focus on clarity, unity, and coherence

- use transitional words from page 46

Title: _____

_____

_____

_____

_____

_____

_____

_____

_____

_____

_____

_____

_____

_____

_____

_____

_____

Activity 16   Peer Editing

Exchange with a classmate the paragraph you wrote in Activity 15. Use Peer Editing Sheet 2 on page 163. Be sure to offer positive suggestions and comments that will help the writer to write a better paragraph. Consider your classmate's comments as you revise your paragraph.

Online Study Center   For more practice, go to the *Great Paragraphs to Great Essays* website at http://esl.college.hmco.com/students

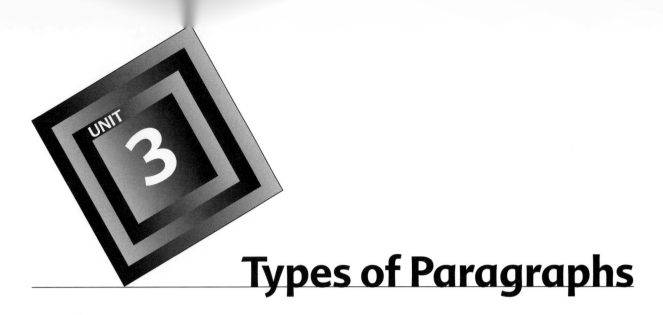

Types of Paragraphs

Writing Goal:	Understanding four types of paragraphs
Language Focus 5:	Subject-verb agreement
Language Focus 6:	Word forms
Examples:	Paragraphs 15–20

In Units 1 and 2, we saw examples of eight different kinds of paragraphs: process, description, narrative, definition, opinion, cause-effect, compare-contrast, and classification. Based on the names of these types of writing, can you guess what kind of information you would find in each?

We use different types of paragraphs to say different things to our readers. For example, if we wanted to talk about the similarities or differences between two cars, we would use a compare-contrast paragraph. If we wanted to describe how to use a microscope, we would use a process paragraph.

In this unit, we will study four types of paragraphs: description, compare-contrast, cause-effect, and classification. In later units, we will study essays of these same types.

Each type of paragraph differs from the others in its form and purpose. Good writers know the different forms and are prepared to write about different topics for different purposes. As you study these four types of paragraphs, pay special attention to the characteristics or features of each one.

DESCRIPTION PARAGRAPHS

Purpose: A description paragraph gives the reader a visual picture of the topic. It gives a point of view about how something looks, feels, tastes, smells, or sounds. The writer's goal is to involve readers so that they can experience the idea or event through the text.

Key Features: A description paragraph has the following features:

- describes

- gives impressions, ideas, or feelings about something

- does not define

- paints a picture for the reader—shows with words

- uses sensory words that appeal to the five senses: hearing, taste, touch, sight, smell

Uses: A description paragraph can be used to do the following things:

- give the features or characteristics of something

- give impressions about something

- give feelings about something

Activity 1   **Analyzing a Description Paragraph**

Read the following description paragraph. Answer the questions that follow.

Paragraph 15

Four Unforgettable Days

I will never forget the Christmas of 2001 when my hometown in New York State was hit by one of the worst winter storms in its history. Blinding snow storms attacked Buffalo and its surrounding suburbs for four consecutive days. The snow fell so hard that I could not see my car parked in my driveway or my neighbor's house across the street. When I tried to drive to a friend's house during a temporary lull in the storm, I had to drive with my head out the side window because I could not see through the foggy windshield. The snow hit my face like miniature bullets, and icicles formed in my hair. In fact, the snow fell so hard that, while most storms are measured in inches, this one was measured in feet. By the time the storm finally let up four days later, more than seven feet of snow had fallen. What I saw when I opened my second story bedroom window shocked me. My entire neighborhood had disappeared under a thick, white blanket of snow! As I looked out the open window, my breath visible in the cool, crisp air, I could not see a single car or bush. Everything was completely buried. I was glad when the snowplows cleared the streets and we were able to return to our normal routines.

blinding: vision blocking

lull: quiet or calm period

icicles: ice formations

let up: stop

snowplows: trucks that clear the streets of snow

1. What is the topic of this paragraph?

   _____

2. Underline the topic sentence and circle the controlling idea.

3. What is the writer's purpose in writing this paragraph?

   _____

4. What do you think the writer's purpose statement was? Write it here.

   _____

5. What features of a description paragraph do you see in this paragraph? Put
   a check next to the feature and then explain your answer.

_____ a. describes _____

_____

_____ b. gives impressions, ideas, or feelings about something _____

_____

_____ c. does not define _____

_____

_____ d. paints a picture for the reader—shows with words _____

_____

_____ e. uses sensory words that appeal to the five senses: hearing, taste, touch, sight, smell

_____

_____

WRITER'S NOTE: Use of *I* in Academic Writing

In general, good writers do not use the pronoun *I* in formal academic writing.
However, the most obvious exception to this is in writing about personal experiences.
The writer paints a picture with words, and very often the writer appears in the
writing, such as in paragraph 15. There is no other way to express *I* except with *I*.
However, do not use *I* in other kinds of academic writing without consulting your
teacher first.

Writing a Description Paragraph

Now it is your turn to write a description paragraph. As you write, keep in mind
everything you learned about the parts of a paragraph in Unit 1, pages 23–24, and the
five elements of good writing in Unit 2.

Activity 2 | **Description Paragraph Practice**

Complete the following items and write a description paragraph.

1. First, brainstorm a topic and then brainstorm ideas for that topic. Here are some topics to choose from, or you may come up with your own topic:

   Describe your house
   Tell about the features of your new cell phone
   Describe how you felt when . . .
   Give your impression of . . .

   Your topic: _____

Brainstorming Box

2. Audience: _____

3. Person (first, second, or third): _____

4. Purpose statement: _____

   _____

5. Topic sentence (with controlling idea): _____

   _____

6. Supporting details (list two to four): _____

_____

_____

Remember to use words that appeal to the five senses.

Title: _____

_____

_____

_____

_____

_____

_____

_____

_____

Activity 3 ⬛ **Peer Editing**

Exchange with a classmate the paragraph you wrote in Activity 2. Use Peer Editing Sheet 3 on page 165. Be sure to offer positive suggestions and comments that will help the writer to create a better paragraph. Consider your classmate's comments as you revise your paragraph.

COMPARE-CONTRAST PARAGRAPHS

Purpose: A compare-contrast essay shows the similarities and/or differences between two people, things, or ideas.

Key Features: A compare-contrast paragraph has the following features:

- two subjects

- compared similarities or contrasted differences

- similarities or differences that are not so obvious

- point-by-point method or block method (These methods are described in Unit 5, pages 96–98.)

Uses: A compare-contrast paragraph may show the following:

- similarities between two things

- differences between two things

- strengths and weaknesses of something

- advantages and disadvantages of something

| Activity 4 | Analyzing a Compare-Contrast Paragraph |

Read the following compare-contrast paragraph. Answer the questions that follow.

Paragraph 16

EXAMPLE PARAGRAPH

Writing and Dancing

On the surface, writers and ballerinas seem to have nothing in common. In reality, the qualities of a good writer <u>mirror</u> the qualities of a good ballerina. One such quality is motivation. Good writers are motivated to learn new and better ways of telling a story, just as ballerinas try to learn many new and better ways of performing certain steps. Another similarity between the two is the importance of dedication. Good writers spend hours each day developing their vocabulary and grammar skills. Likewise, good ballerinas spend countless hours in the gym or studio each week increasing their <u>accuracy</u> and <u>endurance</u>. Finally, people in both professions hope to entertain their audience. Writers choose their themes and language with their audience in mind, and ballerinas consider which steps and which outfits will have the biggest impact on their audience. In sum, few people realize that writers and ballerinas share these common <u>traits</u>.

mirror: to resemble

accuracy: correctness, exact

endurance: stamina, ability to continue

traits: characteristics

1. What is the topic of this paragraph?

_____

_____

2. Underline the topic sentence. (Hint: It is not the first sentence.) Circle the controlling idea.

3. Underline the concluding sentence.

4. What type of concluding sentence is used? (circle one)

   restatement / suggestion / opinion / prediction

5. What is the writer's purpose in writing this paragraph?

   _____

   _____

6. Write what you think the writer's purpose statement was.

   _____

   _____

7. What features of a compare-contrast paragraph do you see in this paragraph?
   Put a check next to the feature and then explain your answer.

   _____ a. two subjects _____

   _____

   _____ b. compared or contrasted _____

   _____

8. Which use of a compare-contrast paragraph did the writer choose? Put a check
   next to the correct answer and then explain your choice.

   a. _____ show the similarities between two things

   b. _____ show the differences between two things

   c. _____ show strengths and weaknesses of something

   d. _____ show advantages and disadvantages of something

   Explanation: _____

   _____

Writing a Compare-Contrast Paragraph

Now it is your turn to write a compare-contrast paragraph. As you write, keep in mind everything you learned about the parts of a paragraph in Unit 1 and the elements of good writing in Unit 2.

Activity 5   Compare-Contrast Paragraph Practice

Complete the following items and then write a paragraph.

1. First, brainstorm a topic and then brainstorm ideas for that topic. Here are some topics to choose from, or come up with your own topic:

   The similarities between high school and college
   The differences between swimming in a pool and at the beach
   The advantages and disadvantages of mandatory voting

   Your topic: _____

Brainstorming Box

2. Audience: _____

3. Person (first, second, or third): _____

4. Purpose statement: _____

_____

5. Topic sentence (with controlling idea): _____

_____

6. Supporting details (list two to four): _____

_____

Title: _____

_____

_____

_____

_____

_____

_____

_____

_____

_____

_____

Activity 6

Peer Editing

Exchange with a classmate the paragraph you wrote in Activity 5. Use Peer Editing Sheet 4 on page 167. Be sure to offer positive suggestions and comments that will help the writer to write a better paragraph. Consider your classmate's comments as you revise your paragraph.

Language Focus 5: Subject-Verb Agreement

All sentences in English contain a verb. The regular present tense has two forms: the base form and the *-s* form. For example, here are the two forms of the verb *write*:

> *write*   I write. They write.

> *writes*   He writes.

The *-s* form is used for third person singular (*he, she, it*).

One of the most common mistakes for nonnative writers is to omit the *-s* in the present tense. Another common mistake is to write *-s* when the verb is not third person singular. This is an error in subject-verb agreement. The form of the verb depends on the subject of the sentence. If you first find the subject, you can write the verb correctly.

Sometimes students are confused because of the opposite ways in which verbs and nouns are made plural. We usually add "s" to a noun to make it plural: 1 cat – 2 cats. However we add "s" to a verb to make it singular: I read – she reads.

Another common subject-verb agreement mistake involves prepositional phrases. A prepositional phrase includes a preposition (for example, *for, at, from, by, with, without, in, of*) and the noun or pronoun that follows.

> The owner <u>of these restaurants</u> is Italian.
>   ↑   ↑
> (preposition: *of*; noun: *restaurants*)

The noun in a prepositional phrase does not affect the number (singular or plural) of the verb in the sentence. Some students choose the form of the verb by looking at the nearest noun. Remember that *the noun in a prepositional phrase is NEVER the subject of a sentence.*

Study the following examples. In each sentence, the subject is underlined once, the verb is in bold type, and the prepositional phrase is italicized. Notice that the verb agrees with the subject, even when the noun in the prepositional phrase comes between the subject and the verb.

> The main <u>product</u> *of Brazil* **is** coffee.

> The main <u>product</u> *of Brazil and Colombia* **is** coffee.

> The main <u>products</u> *of Brazil* **are** coffee and aluminum.

Here are four sentences that nonnative students wrote. Can you identify the mistakes and correct them?

1. In my country, most people lives near the coast because the interior is too dry.

2. When making a decision about what to do, the morals of a person is very important.

3. Sometimes parents and children does not agree on what is best for the children.

4. People say that the airline industry is in trouble and airlines face many economic problems, but all of the flights on my recent vacation trip was full.

Answers: 1. lives ➔ live   2. is ➔ are   3. does ➔ do   4. was ➔ were

Activity 7   **Editing for Subject-Verb Agreement**

Read this paragraph about cloning. Find the two errors in subject-verb agreement. Underline the errors and write the corrections above them.

Paragraph 17

EXAMPLE PARAGRAPH

I understand that many people have different opinions, but I do not understand why there are so much disagreement about cloning. Cloning can be beneficial in many obvious and less than obvious ways. One example of these ways is with disease treatment. Scientists believe that cloning might help us to understand diseases better. If some diseases is stopped, then I think cloning is a good thing. Cloning has a good potential to help human beings, so we should not hesitate to explore this further.

Language Focus 6: Word Forms

One word may have several forms, depending on whether it is a noun, verb, adjective, or adverb. For example, **move** is a verb, but **movement** is a noun. Not all words have all four of these forms. Here are some examples:

NOUN	VERB	ADJECTIVE	ADVERB
difference	differ	different	differently
quickness	X	quick	quickly
repetition	repeat	repeated, repetitive	repeatedly, repetitively

Activity 8   **Editing for Errors in Word Form**

Read this paragraph about capital punishment. They contain six errors in word form. Underline the errors and write the correct form above them.

Paragraph 18

EXAMPLE PARAGRAPH

When I consider capital punishment, I have to admit that I do not agreement with it. Although it is truth that some people will not commit a crime because they are afraid of capital punishment, I am not sure that this is the best way to handle this situation. What is the main reason that I am against capital punish? In most cases, it is impossibly to know whether someone is guilt or not. The government can make mistakes, which means that an innocence person can be killed. That is a mistake that cannot be rectified.

CAUSE-EFFECT PARAGRAPHS

Purpose: A cause-effect paragraph explains the reasons something happens or the results or consequences of an action.

Key Features: A cause-effect paragraph has the following features:

- causes of a thing or event (focus on causes method)
- results of a thing or event (focus on effects method)
- one cause ➔ multiple results
- multiple causes ➔ one result

Uses: A cause-effect paragraph can be used to show the following:

- the causes of something
- the consequences, or effects, of something

Note: Make sure that the topic you choose has a cause-effect relationship.

| Activity 9 | Analyzing a Cause-Effect Paragraph |

Read the following cause-effect paragraph. Answer the questions that follow.

Paragraph 19

EXAMPLE PARAGRAPH

Clinical Depression

How many times have you heard the phrase "I am feeling depressed today"? People tend to misuse the term *depression* to refer to the normal ups and downs of daily life. In reality, depression is a serious illness that can be caused by many factors. Perhaps the most common cause of depression is genetics. People who are born with low levels of serotonin and dopamine cannot experience pleasure in the same way that balanced people can. People with low levels of these substances do not experience happiness from typically happy events. Another cause of depression is alcohol or drug abuse. When drugs enter the bloodstream, they alter the brain's normal chemical balance. Because of this, people who use these chemical substances may experience short-term or long-term depression. Finally, environmental factors can cause clinical depression. Failed relationships, traumatic events, or an abusive childhood can trigger depression. Regardless of its cause, depression is an illness that needs to be taken seriously.

1. What is the topic of this paragraph?

   _____

2. Underline the topic sentence. (Hint: It is not the first sentence.) Circle the controlling idea.

3. Underline the concluding sentence.

4. What type of concluding sentence is used? (circle one)

   restatement / suggestion / opinion / prediction

5. What is the writer's purpose in writing this paragraph?

   _____

6. What do you think the writer's purpose statement was? Write it here.

   _____

   _____

7. What features of a cause-effect paragraph do you see in this paragraph? Put a check next to the feature and then explain your answer on the line that follows.

   _____ a. causes of a thing or event _____

   _____

   _____ b. results of a thing or event _____

   _____

   _____ c. one cause ➔ multiple results _____

   _____

   _____ d. multiple causes ➔ one result _____

   _____

Writing a Cause-Effect Paragraph

   Now it is your turn to write a cause-effect paragraph. As you write, keep in mind everything you learned about the parts of a paragraph in Unit 1 and the elements of good writing in Unit 2.

Activity 10   Cause-Effect Paragraph Practice

Complete the following items and write a cause-effect paragraph.

1. First, brainstorm a topic and then brainstorm ideas for that topic. Here are some topics to choose from, or come up with your own topic:

   • The effects of winning the lottery

   • The causes of car accidents

   • The effects of bad parenting

   Your topic: _____

Brainstorming Box

2. Audience: _____

3. Person (first, second, or third): _____

4. Purpose statement: _____

   _____

5. Topic sentence (with controlling idea): _____

   _____

6. Supporting details (list two to four): _____

   _____

As you write, be sure you have already chosen either a focus-on-causes or a focus-on-effects format.

Title: _____

_____

_____

_____

_____

_____

_____

Activity 11 — Peer Editing

Exchange the paragraph you wrote in Activity 10 with a classmate. Use Peer Editing Sheet 5 on page 169. Be sure to offer positive suggestions and comments that will help the writer to write a better paragraph. Consider your classmate's comments as you revise your paragraph.

CLASSIFICATION PARAGRAPHS

Purpose: A classification paragraph separates ideas into specific categories. It gives the distinguishing or identifying characteristics of something through specific details and examples.

Key Features: A classification paragraph has the following features:

- a thing being classified
- different groups
- distinct categories with no overlap
- descriptions
- identifying characteristics

Uses: A classification paragraph can be used to do the following:

- show the different types or categories of something
- differentiate between the parts of something

Note: In a classification paragraph, the controlling idea distinguishes the individual parts of the whole subject.

Activity 12 — Analyzing a Classification Paragraph

Read the following classification paragraph. Answer the questions that follow.

Paragraph 20

EXAMPLE PARAGRAPH

Runners

In the world of track and field, there are three different types of runners: sprinters, middle distance runners, and distance runners. Sprinters run the shortest distances, in which the races usually last just a few seconds. Sprinters are generally characterized by fast, explosive muscles. These runners are typically extremely muscular. The second type, middle distance runners, run races such as the quarter-mile dash or the 800-meter run. A good middle distance runner must be <u>versatile</u>; he or she must possess a combination of speed and endurance. Physically speaking, a distance runner is on the other end of the <u>spectrum</u> from a sprinter. The final type is the distance runner. He or she typically runs races that are anywhere from 1,600 to 10,000 meters long and has a thin, <u>lean</u> muscle tone. Distance runners are usually small and light. Because their races are longer and take more time to complete, distance runners need to be mentally strong so that they can put forth their best performance over the <u>duration</u> of the race. Because of the variations, almost anyone can fit into one of the three running categories.

versatile: well-rounded, adaptable   **lean:** very little fat
spectrum: range   **duration:** length of time

1. What is the topic of this paragraph?

_____

2. Underline the topic sentence. Circle the controlling idea.

3. Underline the concluding sentence.

4. What type of concluding sentence is used? (circle one)

   restatement / suggestion / opinion / prediction

5. What is the writer's purpose in writing this paragraph?

_____

6. Write what you think the writer's purpose statement was.

_____

_____

7. What features of a classification paragraph do you see in this paragraph? Put a
   check next to the feature and then explain your answer.

_____ a. a thing being classified _____

_____

_____ b. different groups _____

_____

_____ c. distinct categories with no overlap _____

_____

_____ d. identifying characteristics _____

_____

Writing a Classification Paragraph

Now it is your turn to write a classification paragraph. As you write, keep in mind
everything you learned about the parts of a paragraph in Unit 1 and the elements of good
writing in Unit 2.

Activity 13 | **Classification Paragraph Practice**

Complete the items below and write a classification paragraph.

1. First, brainstorm a topic and then brainstorm ideas for that topic. Here are
   some topics to choose from, or come up with your own topic:

   Classify the different types of cars.

   Describe the different types of students on a campus.

   Classify the different types of office jobs.

   Your topic: _____

Brainstorming Box

2. Audience: _____

3. Person (first, second, or third): _____

4. Purpose statement: _____

_____

5. Topic sentence (with controlling idea): _____

_____

6. Supporting details (list two to four): _____

_____

Title: _____

_____

_____

_____

_____

_____

_____

_____

Activity 14 | Peer Editing

Exchange with a classmate the paragraph you wrote in Activity 13. Use Peer Editing Sheet 6 on page 171. Be sure to offer positive suggestions and comments that will help the writer to write a better paragraph. Consider your classmate's comments as you revise your paragraph.

WRITER'S NOTE: Remember the Purpose of Your Paragraph

Before you begin writing, be sure you remember what the focus of your paragraph is. Are you going to describe something (description), show the reasons for or effects of something (cause-effect), or explain the parts of something (classification)? Reread your topic sentence. If the purpose is not clear in the topic sentence, change it so that your readers will know what to expect in the paragraph.

Activity 15 | Identifying Types of Paragraphs

Go back to Units 1 and 2 to find an example for each of these types of paragraphs. Write the title of the paragraph and the page number.

1. **compare-contrast**   Title: _____   Page: _____

2. **description**   Title: _____   Page: _____

3. **cause-effect**   Title: _____   Page: _____

4. **classification**   Title: _____   Page: _____

Online Study Center   For more practice, go to the *Great Paragraphs to Great Essays* website at http://esl.college.hmco.com/students

Moving from Paragraph to Essay

Writing Goals:	Understanding similarities between paragraphs and essays
	Writing a descriptive essay
Language Focus 7:	Describing with the five senses
Language Focus 8:	Prepositions of location
Examples:	Paragraphs 21–32, Essays 1–2

In Units 1–3, we reviewed the basics of paragraph writing. We learned that a paragraph is a group of thoughts about one idea that includes a main subject and a controlling idea.

An **essay** is very similar to a paragraph in its organization and order, but an essay includes more information and depth about a topic. Essays allow the writer to go into more detail about a particular subject. In an essay, each point is presented in an individual paragraph. This means that more examples, explanations, and details can be written about specific **points of development**.

The following chart shows the relationship between the parts of a paragraph and an essay.

	Paragraph	**Essay**	**Function**
Introduction	– – –	• Hook	• Gets readers interested
	• Topic sentence	• Thesis statement	• Gives main idea of the writing
Body	• Supporting sentences	• Topic sentences of paragraphs	• Give details of the main idea
	– – –	• Supporting sentences of paragraphs	• Explain the topic sentences of an essay
Conclusion	• Concluding sentence	• Concluding paragraph	• Signals the end of the writing

REVIEWING PARAGRAPH BASICS

Descriptive Paragraphs and Essays

Activity 1   **Studying a Sample Paragraph**

Read and study the following descriptive paragraph. Work with a partner to answer the questions before and after the paragraph. These questions will help you to understand the content and the organization of the paragraph.

1. Have you ever worked in an office? If so, describe the office where you worked.

   _____

   _____

   _____

2. How do you imagine the ideal office should look? _____

   _____

   _____

   _____

Paragraph 21

My Daily Prison

I often get the impression that my workplace is a prison. For instance, the level of security at my customer service company is incredible. I have to <u>punch in</u> a special code to enter the parking lot; then the security guard carefully examines my <u>badge</u> even though he has seen me every day for the past ten years! The cafeteria also reminds me of prison. When it is time for lunch, I look around at the dark gray walls. There are no pictures hanging there, just a thin layer of grease. We line up and <u>shuffle</u> slowly through the line, hoping for a new recipe. However, we get <u>wilted</u> salad, lumpy mashed potatoes with salty gravy, or a fatty chicken thigh. After lunch, I head back to my closed-in <u>cubicle</u> and wait for our conference meeting time. It is always the same. The supervisor enters and reads off, in a robotic voice, the latest company problems and concerns. We sit quietly, not allowed to speak. After the meeting, I go back to work on the <u>chain gang</u>. Time seems to stand still in my prisonlike workplace, but I always manage to make it to 5:00 p.m.

punch in: enter numbers using a keypad

badge: identification card, usually containing a photograph

shuffle: walk slowly while dragging your feet

wilted: limp, not fresh

cubicle: a small workspace usually made out of temporary or movable walls

chain gang: traditionally, a group of prisoners, connected by chains around their ankles, doing hard labor outdoors

3. Underline the topic sentence and circle the controlling idea.

4. List at least three general examples of how the writer's workplace is similar to a prison.

_____

_____

Activity 2 | Studying a Sample Essay

Now read a descriptive essay that is based on the paragraph in Activity 1. Answer the questions that follow.

Essay 1

EXAMPLE ESSAY

Prisoner at Work

I am not a criminal. I am an honest, hard-working individual who follows the laws and stays out of trouble. However, I can imagine what a prison feels like. All I have to do is think about the customer service company where I work. From the time I arrive at work to the time I leave, I get the <u>distinct</u> impression that I am <u>indeed</u> in prison.

Paragraph 22

Before I even enter my building at 9:00 a.m., I get the feeling that I am entering a high-security building. I punch in a special code to enter the parking lot. The cold metallic arm slowly <u>swings</u> up, allowing me to pass. As I get out of my car and <u>proceed</u> toward the entrance, I must prepare my badge for inspection. A <u>stern</u> guard wearing a black and white uniform takes a look at my photo and <u>glances</u> up at my face. I have seen him every day for the past ten years, yet he continues to do this as if he has never laid eyes on me before! After successfully getting past the guard, I enter the lobby of my building. I must then empty my purse of all sharp objects such as keys and nail files. I walk through the metal detector, and if I am lucky, the alarm does not sound. I walk down the <u>frigid</u> hallway until I come to a steel door with a sign that says, "Authorized personnel only." My ten-digit number must be punched in correctly for the door to open. I am relieved when the light shines green and I can enter on the first try.

Paragraph 23

My workday has begun, and I know that it will follow the same routine as every other day. As I get to my dull cubicle, I look around and see that all my co-workers' cubicles are exactly like mine. Like prison cells, they are the same size, decorated the same way, and separated from each other by <u>partitions</u>. From 9:00 a.m. to 9:30, I answer the usual e-mails from other employees. After that, I get busy with my telephone work. When customers call in, I have a "speech" that I read to them. There is no creativity on my part. I cannot <u>veer</u> from the company's statement. Just like a prisoner, I have no freedom of speech.

Paragraph 24

My lunchtime routine never changes either. At 12:30, we all proceed to the cafeteria. The moment we walk in, we are bombarded by the powerful smell of fried food and grease. I look around and see that the cafeteria decor has not changed. The walls are lifeless and gray. There are no pictures or other wall hangings, just a thin layer of grease. We line up and move through the line slowly, hoping for a new recipe. Alas, the food choices are the same as usual: wilted salad, lumpy mashed potatoes with salty gravy, and a fatty chicken thigh. The most colorful item in the food line is the dessert, jiggly Jell-O, but I never pick up a bowl. That would really mean that I was in prison . . . or a hospital!

Paragraph 25

Thirty minutes later, we are back in our cubicles, preparing for our afternoon meetings. The enormous conference room contains an oval conference table with twenty shabby chairs. Like clockwork, the supervisor enters at precisely the same time each day. She reads through her routine list of problems and concerns. As employees, we do not speak. We sit like prisoners and listen to our "warden's" robotic voice telling us what we are doing well and what we are doing wrong. We are also given reports to fill out during these meetings. There is no room for creativity in these reports. The multiple-choice answers require only a quick check mark. After that, I go back to work on the chain gang. I answer phone calls, input information in the computer, and glance at my watch. Time seems to stand still, but somehow, I always make it to 5 p.m.

Paragraph 26

That's my professional life. I make a good living, and my salary allows me to live comfortably. However, the atmosphere is oppressive. I walk into my office building, and my creative thought processes shut down. This mindless feeling continues until I drive out of the parking lot. If I were a stronger person, perhaps I would think about changing careers. However, everyone knows the stories of prisoners who are finally released from jail. Many of them find that they miss the routines of a prison, and they end up going back.

Paragraph 27

distinct: clear; unmistakable

indeed: in fact; in reality

swings: moves

proceed: move forward; enter

stern: strict

glances: looks at quickly

frigid: very cold

partitions: wall-like barriers, usually temporary

veer: change: move away from

Jell-O: a fruit-flavored gelatin dessert

shabby: worn, run-down

stand still: not move

oppressive: restrictive; limiting

end up: result in

1. What is the main idea of the essay?

   _____

   _____

2. Find the sentence in Paragraph 23 that is similar to the topic sentence of "My Daily Prison." Write it here.

   _____

   _____

   (The key sentence in a paragraph is the topic sentence. In an essay, a similar key sentence is called the thesis statement.)

WRITER'S NOTE: The Hook

Do you know what a hook is? A hook is what a fisherman uses to catch a fish. In writing, a hook is a sentence or sentences that catch the reader's attention. It gives the reader a reason to keep reading the essay. It is important to remember that the hook should not be the main idea or the thesis of the essay.

3. Reread paragraphs 23–26 of the essay. Underline the topic sentence in each of these paragraphs.

4. In the introductory paragraph (Paragraph 22), what is the hook (how does the writer describe herself)?

_____

5. The writer uses many adjectives to help describe her job. Find the adjectives that describe these nouns:

   a. guard (Paragraph 23) _____

   b. cubicle (Paragraph 24) _____

   c. layer (Paragraph 25) _____

   d. food (Paragraph 25) _____

   e. conference room (Paragraph 26) _____

6. Reread the conclusion (Paragraph 27). How does the writer connect the conclusion of the essay to the introduction (hook) of the essay?

_____

Outlining a Descriptive Essay

Working with an outline after you have read an essay helps you to see the essay's structure.

Activity 3   **Completing a Descriptive Essay Outline**

Study the incomplete outline below of "Prisoner at Work," pages 74–75, and fill in the missing information.

   I. Introduction (Paragraph 22)

      A. Hook: _comparison to criminals_____

      B. Connecting information: _imagining life as a prisoner_____

      C. Thesis: _____

II. Body

    A. Paragraph 23 topic sentence: ___Before I even enter my building at 9:00 a.m., I get the___

    ___feeling that I am entering a high-security building___

        1. _____

           a. ___Metallic arm___

           b. ___Allows me to pass___

        2. ___A stern guard is waiting for me.___

           a. _____

           b. _____

           c. ___He does the same thing every day.___

        3. _____

           a. ___I empty my purse.___

           b. ___I walk through the metal detector and down the hallway.___

           c. _____

    B. Paragraph 24 topic sentence: _____

    _____

        1. ___Describe my cubicle___

           a. _____

           b. ___Same size as everyone else's, same decorations___

        2. ___My morning routine___

           a. ___Answer e-mails___

           b. _____

           c. ___No freedom of speech___

C. Paragraph 25 topic sentence: <u>My lunchtime routine never changes either.</u>

   1. _____

   2. <u>Cafeteria walls are lifeless and gray</u>

   3. _____

   4. <u>We line up for the food.</u>

D. Paragraph 26 topic sentence: <u>Thirty minutes later, we are back in our cubicle, preparing for</u>
   <u>our afternoon meetings.</u>

   1. <u>Conference room</u>

      a. _____

      b. _____

      c. <u>Given reports to fill out</u>

   2. <u>Back to the office</u>

      a. _____

      b. _____

III. Conclusion (Paragraph 27)

   A. <u>Restate my job and describe the atmosphere</u>

   B. <u>Connect it to prisoners' lives</u>

LANGUAGE FOCUS 7: Describing with the Five Senses

It is important for a writer to use vocabulary that gives the reader the information as vividly and clearly as possible. Very good writers use words that appeal to the five senses: sight, taste, touch, hearing, and smell. By using these senses, the writer *shows* rather than *tells* the idea of the essay. Compare these examples:

Poor: The boy entered the room. He was very tired.

Better: The boy entered the room, and we heard the thud as his body collapsed on the floor.

Poor: His clothing was dirty.

Better: First, I saw that his clothing was dirty, but then I noticed that the air around him reminded me of sour milk.

Activity 4 | Focusing on Sense Words

Study the nouns on the left. Write three adjectives to describe each noun. The first one has been done for you. When you have finished, compare answers with your classmates' answers. Can you classify your adjectives as appealing to one or more of the five senses?

1. a park   littered   lush   green

2. a wedding dress _____ _____ _____

3. a puppy _____ _____ _____

4. a cup of soup _____ _____ _____

5. a professor _____ _____ _____

6. a pop singer _____ _____ _____

7. a car _____ _____ _____

8. a party _____ _____ _____

9. a university _____ _____ _____

10. a book _____ _____ _____

Two Ways to Organize Descriptive Essays

Commonly, descriptive essays are organized according to time (in what order things happen) or space (what is seen from left to right, top to bottom, etc.).

Activity 5 | Organizing with Time

Reread "Prisoner at Work," pages 74–75. How does the writer use time to organize the information in the essay?

_____

_____

Activity 6	Organizing with Space

Study the following essay. It describes a restaurant using spatial organization. Then work with a partner to draw a sketch showing the placement of what the writer describes. Use separate paper.

Essay 2

EXAMPLE ESSAY

The Restaurant

On any given weekend, young people get together for a night of fun. Friends gather to go to the movies, to a local club, or to a trendy restaurant. These are normal activities, but not for me. I am a server. While my friends are socializing at parties or in restaurants, I work in the dining room of a popular nightspot. It is 11:00 p.m., and I scan the restaurant and take in all the action: people from all walks of life interacting with each other.

Paragraph 28

In the left corner of the restaurant are the round tables, and at this moment, they are all occupied. At one table, I can see a group of four young, attractive women. They are all laughing heartily. I think the leader of the group has just finished telling a joke. These young women are wearing brightly colored career outfits; they probably decided to go out directly after work. It is, in fact, a Friday night. To the right of the women sits a couple. I am not sure whether they are married or not. It is too dark to notice if their fingers have rings on them. Whatever their relationship is, they are definitely arguing. They are hunched forward, and their faces are tense. Perhaps they do not want others in the restaurant to hear what they are fighting about. The man is holding onto his glass tightly. The woman is tearing her napkin into tiny pieces. I am glad I cannot hear what they are saying; their body language tells me enough.

Paragraph 29

In the bar area, other things are happening. Two people in their thirties are sitting directly in front of the bartender. They look happy to be here. They whisper into each other's ear and smile as if they are keeping secrets from the rest of the world. He is elegantly dressed in a cashmere sweater, and she is wearing a flowing Indian print dress. Each of them, in turn, touches the other's forearm from time to time, perhaps to emphasize a particular point. Next to them, a middle-aged man is sitting alone. I can smell his top-of-the-line cologne whenever I pass by as I head to the kitchen. Although he is alone, he is definitely not lonely. His state-of-the-art cell phone has not left his ear since he came in. I cannot tell whether his phone call is business or pleasure because he alternates from serious tones to lighthearted chuckles. Every once in a while, he asks the bartender to refresh his drink. The clinking of the ice, however, is drowned out by the music coming from the dance floor.

Paragraph 30

The dance floor is to the right of the dining area, and it is filled with all sorts of people, young and old. A group of women is dancing in a circle. These women look as though they might be co-workers of the women sitting at the other end of the restaurant, but I am not sure. One of them has her eyes closed and is <u>swaying</u> to the hard dance beat. Near the circle, a man is trying to feel the <u>rhythm</u> himself. He is older, but he is trying to look young and trendy. Dressed completely in black, he is dancing while <u>staring</u> at his feet. The beat of the <u>bass</u> gets faster, and he <u>jerks</u> his head up. Without warning, he <u>stomps</u> off the dance floor. Mixed in with these people, of course, are the couples. They dance close together, although the music does not necessarily lend itself to that style of dancing. They are young, no doubt, and will continue to dance that way all night long.

Paragraph 31

This is my job. I take food orders and watch people, from the couples fighting to the others having a good time on the dance floor. I do not pretend to be a psychologist, but it is interesting to watch people interact. My job might not be the most socially rewarding job in the world, but every night I learn something new about human nature. *That* makes me happy.

Paragraph 32

trendy: popular and in-style

scan: to examine something from one point to another

heartily: deeply

hunched: bent forward

tense: rigid; serious

whisper: to speak softly

cashmere: a soft, expensive type of wool

flowing: moving (like a river)

in turn: one by one

top-of-the-line: the best quality

head to: move in the direction of

state-of-the-art: modern; the latest model

lighthearted: happy; not serious

clinking: a sound that is made when two objects, such as glasses, hit each other

drown out: to overpower a sound with a louder sound

sway: move gently back and forth

rhythm: a consistent beat (of music)

stare at: to look at intently

bass: deep notes (of music)

jerk: pull sharply

stomps: to hit the floor hard with your foot

LANGUAGE FOCUS 8: Prepositions of Place

To clearly describe a situation or event using spatial organization, writers often use prepositions of location. Study the following list.

above	*across*	*along*	*at*	*below*
between	*by*	*inside*	*near*	*on*
next to	*in front of*	*to the right of*		

Activity 7	Prepositions of Place

Look around your classroom. Write four original sentences based on what you see. Use prepositions of place from Language Focus 8. In addition, try to use vivid adjectives in your sentences.

1. _____

2. _____

3. _____

4. _____

EIGHT STEPS IN WRITING AN ESSAY

**"True ease in writing
comes from art, not chance,
as those move easiest
who have learned to dance."**

-Alexander Pope

What this famous quote means is that great writers are not born but acquire their skill through practice. The following section will show you the process that many writers follow when they write an essay.

No writers, not even professionals, sit down and write an essay from the introduction to the conclusion. Effective writers approach an essay as many small pieces of writing that are done step by step. Now that you have learned the fundamentals of paragraphs, moving on to the essay is easy. An essay is just a collection of paragraphs, organized much like an individual paragraph with an introduction, a body, and a conclusion. In this section, you will learn how to write an essay step-by step, paragraph-by-paragraph.

A five-paragraph essay can be broken down into the following parts:

1. **Introduction** paragraph: Includes hook, connecting ideas, thesis (with **points of development**)

2. First **body** paragraph: Topic sentence, supporting details, (concluding/ transitional sentence)

3. Second **body** paragraph: Topic sentence, supporting details, (concluding/ transitional sentence)

4. Third **body** paragraph: Topic sentence, supporting details, (concluding/ transitional sentence)

5. **Conclusion** paragraph: Restatement of thesis and points of development; suggestion, opinion, or prediction

As you can see, an essay is a collection of five related paragraphs, constructed to work together.

Following a series of steps will help you write cohesive essays about many different topics. Study the eight steps below and answer the questions when prompted to do so.

Step 1: Choose a Topic

You can choose a topic in a couple of ways.

a. *Choose something familiar.* Since writing is an expression of your thoughts and ideas, it is easier to write about something you know well; it is even better to write about something you are passionate or excited about. List at least three things that you know well:

_____

_____

_____

b. *Choose something that you are interested in and want to learn about.* This is a great way to improve your mind, discover a new hobby, or decide if you like something without even doing it. For example, if you have an interest in skydiving but have never done it, you might decide to find information about that topic and then write about it.

_____

_____

_____

Step 2: Brainstorm

Brainstorm ideas for your topic. *Brainstorming* is a term that describes the process writers use to get their ideas about a topic down onto the paper. (See Unit 1, page 11.) There are many ways to brainstorm, and you might already have a preferred method. If not, try each of these and see which works best for you.

a. *Jot down ideas.* Write down everything about the topic that comes to your mind. Your ideas do not have to be in sentence form. Do not worry about grammar, spelling, order, or organization. Just transfer ideas directly from your brain to the paper as fast as they come to you. For example, write down everything you know about lotteries.

_____

_____

_____

b. *Make a web diagram.* Write down an idea, draw a circle around it. Branching off from that idea, draw lines to related ideas. For an essay about the types of horror movies, a web diagram might look like the one below. What examples can you think of if you were to write more details in the chart?

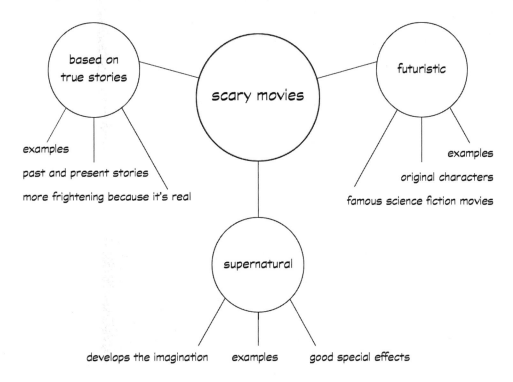

c. *Freewrite.* Freewriting is a technique in which a writer puts pen to paper and writes whatever comes to his or her mind. The idea is to keep writing without stopping. If you drift off topic, that's fine—just keep putting words on paper, and eventually they will be about your topic. This is a great brainstorming technique to use when you are having trouble coming up with ideas. Practice freewriting with this sentence starter:

Yesterday was a terrible day for me because _____

_____

_____

_____

_____

_____

Step 3: Write a Purpose Statement

Ask yourself what the purpose of the essay is. Are you going to describe something? Compare two things? Show cause and effect? Argue a point? Being sure of the purpose will make following the rest of the steps much easier.

Read the following essay titles. What do you think the writer's purpose is?

Title	Purpose
Mountain Bikes Versus Street Bikes	_____
	_____
My First Date	_____
	_____
The Popularity of Video Games	_____
	_____
Stopping Pollution	_____
	_____
Pop Music: Then and Now	_____
	_____

Step 4: Organize and Outline

Organize your ideas. Once you have finished brainstorming, reread what you have written. Do any ideas jump out at you or seem interesting? Circle the things that seem to fit the purpose of your essay. During this step, you must choose how you are going to organize these ideas:

- Chronologically (time order or order of events)

- In spatial order: based on a logical order (what you see)

- In order of importance: the least important idea (reason, example) first, then the second most important one, with the most important idea last. This can also be done in opposite order, with the most important or strongest point of development coming first and ending with the least important.

You can put numbers next to the items you have chosen from your brainstorming to show where they will appear in your essay. Group your ideas into three main categories. These will be the three points of development for your three body paragraphs. Study this example:

A student is writing an essay classifying different types of schooling. She has written down many ideas but has not organized them in logical order. Read her list of ideas and write them down under an appropriate category. Some may belong in more than one category.

school bus in front of your house	reduced lunch prices	various clubs and sports
study at your own pace	few distractions	uniforms
flexible study and relax times	private teachers	teacher release days

Home Schooling   **Public School**   **Private School**

_____   _____   _____

_____   _____   _____

_____   _____   _____

_____   _____   _____

_____   _____   _____

_____   _____   _____

In this step, you also create an outline for your essay. Many writers use the traditional outline format that includes these sections:

> **Introduction** paragraph: with hook, connecting ideas, and thesis statement
>
> First through third **body** paragraphs: with topic sentence, supporting details, (concluding/transitional sentence)
>
> **Conclusion** paragraph: with restatement of thesis and points of development; suggestion, opinion, or prediction

Refer to the outline of "Prisoner at Work" on pages 77–79 for more information.

Step 5: Write a Thesis Statement

From your brainstorming notes and your outline, create a thesis statement for your essay. A thesis tells what your essay is going to be about. In other words, a reader should be able to read your thesis and get a clear idea of what you are trying to accomplish. Refer to your purpose statement when creating your sample thesis.

There are basically two types of thesis statements:

Implied thesis: The main points are not stated.

>   Buying a car is not as easy as it sounds because there are many factors to consider.

Stated thesis: The main points are clearly stated.

>   Buyers should keep in mind many factors when purchasing a car: price, gas mileage, and functionality.

The underlined words are called **points of development**. Many instructors ask their students to use points of development in their thesis. If your instructor does so, create three points of development based on the organization you followed in Step 3. These points of development are the three things that you will use as topic sentences for the three body paragraphs of your essay.

Remember that you may need to change your thesis statement as you work on developing your essay.

Step 6: Develop Supporting Details

Paragraphs can be written in any order. Choose the order that is easiest for you.

Introductory Paragraph

The introductory paragraph consists of the hook and the connecting information, which leads from the hook to the thesis. Study the following example.

> **According to a recent survey, approximately forty-one percent of Americans fear speaking in public.** That statistic places public speaking as the number one phobia in the United States. More than a fear of spiders, death, and the Internal Revenue Service, public speaking is something that often causes people to break out into a cold sweat, start shaking uncontrollably, and even feel as though they are about to die. Fear of public speaking can come from a number of sources, including childhood events and continuous media attention to the problem. Perhaps more important than the causes of this phobia are the strategies for overcoming fear of public speaking. *Many people are unaware that the fear of speaking in front of others can be overcome by visualization exercises, deep breathing, and preparedness.*

hook: beginning of introductory paragraph

connecting information

thesis statement: end of introductory paragraph

Reread the hook. In your opinion, does it catch readers' attention and make them interested in reading further? _____

Why or why not? _____

_____

_____

_____

Now reread the connecting information. Do you see a pattern from general to more specific? _____

Body Paragraphs 1–3

Each of these paragraphs is based on and will explain one of your points of development in the thesis, whether it is stated or implied. The topic sentence will state your point of development for that paragraph.

Supporting detail sentences follow the topic sentence. Remember from Unit 1, pages 12–13, that each supporting sentence has a specific function: to describe, to give reasons, to give facts, to give examples, or to define. Good writers choose wording and placement very carefully to make their meaning clear.

Conclusion Paragraph

The purpose of the conclusion is to recap or summarize for the reader the main idea of the essay. An essay should read just like a typical class period runs. For example, the teacher tells the students what they are going to learn (introductory paragraph, thesis), the teacher then teaches the lesson (body paragraphs, points of development), and finally, the teacher recaps or reviews what he or she taught that day (conclusion, restatement of thesis).

Try restating your thesis in the conclusion. To restate your thesis means that you should write the basic idea of the thesis but in a different way. Effective writers do this to clarify for the reader what was just said.

An effective writer can also restate the points of development in the conclusion. This helps readers to recall the three main points that they just learned about without having to go back and reread the thesis.

Step 7: Write the First Draft

In this step, you develop your outline from Step 4 into a working essay. You expand the thoughts you wrote in the outline into complete sentences. Make sure that you begin a new indented paragraph when you begin writing about new information.

Add Connectors and Transitions

As you write your first draft, or after you finish and look back at it, you can use a simple technique to improve the quality and clarity of your writing: adding connecting and transition words, phrases, or sentences. Using transitions does the following to your writing:

- Improves clarity
- Shows the relationship between ideas
- Improves the flow of the essay
- Connects paragraphs

Remember that transitions can be as small as one word when used at the beginning, middle, or end of a sentence. Use transitional words in sentences to do the following:

Add an idea	*then, next, in addition, moreover, besides, furthermore*
Create contrast	*however, nevertheless, conversely, on the other hand, in contrast*
Emphasize	*above all, especially, in fact, surely, most importantly, equally important*

In some cases, an entire sentence may act as a transition, such as at the end of a body paragraph. These sentences also work well as concluding sentences.

Step 8: Revise Your Essay One or More Times

Because good writing is never accomplished on the first try, it is important to edit your writing and make changes to enhance the essay. You can edit and revise your paper or have a teacher, friend, or family member help you.

Now that you have studied the steps that good writers take in writing an essay, it is time to develop an original piece of writing.

WRITING A DESCRIPTIVE ESSAY

Activity 8   **Completing the Steps**

As you work through this activity, refer to same eight steps above if you need more information.

Step 1: Choose a Topic

Read the list of topics below. Choose one that you like or another topic that your teacher approves. This topic will be the main subject of your descriptive essay.

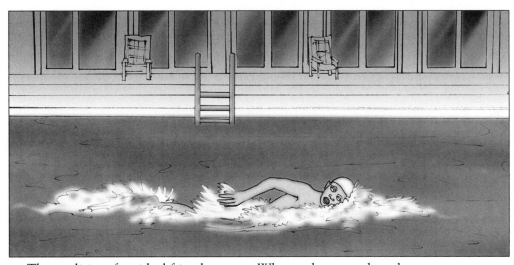

The qualities of an ideal friend   What makes a good teacher

Your favorite place   A major sporting event

General topic: _____

Step 2: Brainstorm

Using a method that works for you, brainstorm ideas about your topic.

Brainstorming Box

Step 3: Write a Purpose Statement

What information do you want to share with your audience and why?

_____

_____

Step 4: Organize and Outline

Based on the brainstorming, decide what information you are going to include in your essay and how it will be organized (chronologically, in spatial order, or in order of importance). Then list your three points of development.

1. _____

2. _____

3. _____

Now write an outline. Use separate paper.

Step 5: Write a Thesis Statement

Will your thesis be stated or implied? Write it here and circle the type.

Thesis statement: _____

_____ (implied / stated)

Step 6: Develop Supporting Details

Go back to the outline you created in Step 4 and add supporting details. Refer to the outline of "Prisoner at Work" on pages 77–79 for examples of supporting information.

Now exchange outlines with another student. Use Peer Editing Sheet 7 on page 173 to make comments about your partner's outline.

Step 7: Write the First Draft

On a separate sheet of paper or on a computer, write the first draft of your essay. Remember to skip lines because it will be easier for you to make changes if you have adequate space.

Be sure to check the transition phrases in your draft for clarity and unity. Look for areas that might need clarification or improved flow and use transition words or phrases there. Try to have at least two transitions in each paragraph.

Step 8: Revise Your Essay One or More Times

Check to make sure that you are using correct vocabulary, punctuation, and clear language in your essay.

Activity 9   **Final Draft Checklist**

Complete the checklist below about the final draft of your essay. If you answer NO to any of the questions, make those necessary changes before turning in your essay.

	Yes	No
1. Did I include a thesis statement that contains a clear topic and points of development?		
2. Is the purpose of my essay clear?		
3. Does each body paragraph have a clear topic sentence?		
4. Are my thoughts and ideas organized clearly in each paragraph?		
5. Did I use a variety of descriptive adjectives?		
6. Are all prepositions used correctly?		
7. Is my use of punctuation correct?		
8. Did I use connecting transition words and expressions correctly?		
9. Does the concluding paragraph have words and phrases that signal the end of the essay?		
10. Is the conclusion free of any new ideas that were not mentioned in the introductory paragraph?		

Activity 10   **Proofreading and Editing Your Work**

Exchange with a classmate the essay that you wrote in Activity 8. Use Peer Editing Sheet 8 on page 175. Be sure to offer positive suggestions and comments that will help the writer to write a better essay.

ADDITIONAL TOPICS FOR WRITING

Here are five more ideas for writing a descriptive essay:

1. Write about the house you grew up in when you were a child. What did it look like? What memories do you have of this house? What impression does this house have on you?

2. Describe a favorite building or kind of architecture. Why do you like it? What effect does it have on you?

3. Describe a family tradition. Write about what happens during this time, who is involved, and what the importance of the tradition is.

4. Describe a very emotional moment or day in your life. Try to include some impressions that you and your friends had that day.

5. Describe the perfect place to relax. How do the characteristics of this place lead to your relaxation?

 **Online Study Center**   For more practice, go to the *Great Paragraphs to Great Essays* website at http://esl.college.hmco.com/students

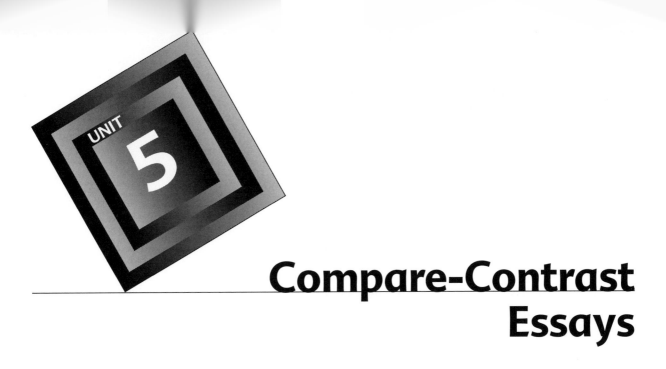

Compare-Contrast Essays

Writing Goal:	Writing compare-contrast essays
Language Focus 9:	Comparative and superlative
Language Focus 10:	Parallel structure
Examples:	Paragraphs 33–43; Essays 3–4

A compare-contrast essay is one of the most common forms of essay writing. In a good compare-contrast essay, the writer discusses two subjects. The subjects can be anything—people, objects, places, or ideas.

In a comparison essay, the writer focuses on similarities. In a contrast essay, the writer focuses on differences. In a compare-contrast essay, the writer focuses on both similarities and differences.

CHOOSING A SUBJECT

The choice of subjects for this kind of essay is crucial. It is possible to compare or contrast many pairs of subjects. In an effective compare-contrast essay, the writer discusses two subjects that do not appear to be similar but are presented in a new way so that readers can see the not-so-obvious similarities. Of course, it is also possible to do the opposite, that is, point out the hidden differences between two subjects that appear very similar on the surface. The writer makes readers think about the two subjects in a new, deeper way. A good essay of this kind does not compare or contrast two obvious subjects. In other words, the writer surprises us by making us rethink our opinion or belief about the two subjects.

Activity 1   **Choose Appropriate Topics and Titles**

Read these ten essay titles. Put an X next to the five that are most appropriate for a compare-contrast essay. Be prepared to defend your choices.

_____ 1. Why People Should Be Vegetarians

_____ 2. Laptop Computers and Personal Computers

_____ 3. The Worst Day of My Professional Life

_____ 4. Cats and Dogs as Pets

_____ 5. Male Bosses and Female Bosses

_____ 6. The Steps in Writing a Successful Resume

_____ 7. Major Personality Types of Young Children

_____ 8. Fast Food Versus Fine Dining

_____ 9. The Unforeseen Effects of Intercontinental Travel

_____ 10. A Comparison of Charles Dickens' book *A Christmas Carol* and the 1999 movie of the same name.

ORGANIZATION OF A COMPARE-CONTRAST ESSAY

Writers organize a compare-contrast essay in two major ways. In the **block method**, the writer discusses characteristics of the first subject and then uses the same characteristics to discuss the second subject. An alternative way is the **point-by-point method**. Here, the writer discusses one characteristic at a time of both subjects. Though other organizational methods are possible, these two are the most common.

Regardless of which method you are using, you must choose characteristics to compare and contrast the two subjects. For example, if your two subjects are life in New York City in 1900 and life in New York City in 2000, you might include these three characteristics in your essay: population, employment, and transportation.

Block Method

In this method, the writer discusses a set of characteristics about one subject first before discussing the same set of characteristics about the second subject. It is important to discuss the characteristics in the same order. Here is an example of an outline using the block method.

"Life in New York City in 1900 and 2000"

I. Introduction

    A. Hook

    B. Connection information

    C. Thesis statement: Though New York City in 1900 was quite different from New York City in 2000 in many ways, important similarities existed in population, employment, and transportation.

II. Life in NYC in 1900   (subject 1)

    A. Population   (characteristic 1)

    B. Employment   (characteristic 2)

    C. Transportation   (characteristic 3)

III. Life in NYC in 2000   (subject 2)

    A. Population   (characteristic 1)

    B. Employment   (characteristic 2)

    C. Transportation   (characteristic 3)

IV. Conclusion

Remember that the purpose of your essay is to clearly point out similarities and/or differences. In the block method, sometimes the specific similarities or differences and the degree of similarity or difference are not so clear. Good writers make sure that readers can see the comparisons and contrasts clearly.

Point-by-Point Method

In the point-by-point method, information about the two subjects is contained within each paragraph, thus making the writer's comparison or contrast much easier for the reader to understand. In this method, the writer discusses one characteristic about both subjects first before discussing the second characteristic about both subjects and then the third characteristic. (You must use at least two characteristics.)

Be sure to discuss the subjects in the same order for each characteristic. Here is an example of an outline using the point-by-point method.

"Life in New York City in 1900 and 2000"

I. Introduction

  A. Hook

  B. Connection information

  C. Thesis statement: Though New York City in 1900 was quite different from New York City in 2000 in many ways, important similarities existed in population, employment, and transportation.

II. Population   (Characteristic 1)

  A. Life in NYC in 1900   (Subject 1)

  B. Life in NYC in 2000   (Subject 2)

III. Employment   (Characteristic 2)

  A. Life in NYC in 1900   (Subject 1)

  B. Life in NYC in 2000   (Subject 2)

IV. Transportation   (Characteristic 3)

  A. Life in NYC in 1900   (Subject 1)

  B. Life in NYC in 2000   (Subject 2)

V. Conclusion

Supporting Details

The essay "Life in New York City in 1900 and 2000" will have supporting sentences for each point of comparison or contrast. For an example of supporting details, we can look at the two characteristics of population and country of birth. The following chart shows how this information is handled in each method of essay organization.

Block Method	Point-by-Point Method

"Life in New York City in 1900 and 2000"
 	
II. Life in NYC in 1900
 	
   A. Population
 	
     1. *Population was 2,000,000; #1 in the U.S.*
 	
     2. *Percentage of foreign-born: 40%*
 	
   B. Employment
 	
   C. Transportation
 	
III. Life in NYC in 2000
 	
   A. Population
 	
     1. *Population was 8,000,000; #1 in the U.S.*
 	
     2. *Percentage of foreign-born: 36%*
 	
   B. Employment
 	
   C. Transportation
	"Life in New York City in 1900 and 2000"
	
	II. Population
	
	   A. Life in NYC in 1900
	
	     1. *Population 2,000,000 and #1 city in the U.S.*
	
	     2. *40% of population was foreign-born*
	
	   B. Life in NYC in 2000
	
	     1. *Population 8,000,000 and #1 city in the U.S.*
	
	     2. *36% of population was foreign-born*

Activity 2   Making an Outline for a Compare-Contrast Essay

Here is an outline for an essay that compares the weather in two cities. The outline is missing important pieces. Use the answers below to fill in the missing pieces.

opinion	Effects	Miami	Temperature
Difference 3	Names of seasons	hurricanes	Introduction
Thesis statement	Restate	Location	Chicago

Title: The Weather in Chicago and Miami

I. _____

    A. Hook

    B. Background Information

    C. _____

II. Difference 1: the number of seasons

    A. Chicago

        1. Location

        2. Number of seasons

        3. Names of seasons

    B. Miami

        1. _____

        2. Number of seasons

        3. _____

III. Difference 2: the worst temperature

    A. _____

        1. Worst season

        2. Temperature (supporting fact)

    B. _____

        1. Worst season

        2. _____ (supporting fact)

IV. _____: bad weather

    A. Chicago

        1. Blizzard

        2. When blizzards occur

        3. _____ of a blizzard

    B. Miami

        1. Hurricane

        2. When _____ occur

        3. Effects of a hurricane

V. Conclusion

    A. _____ the thesis statement

    B. Summarize the main points

    C. Concluding statement: a suggestion, _____, or prediction

Activity 3   **Studying a Sample Paragraph to Essay**

In both the paragraph and the essay that follows, the writer discusses the effects of weather in two popular cities in the United States. The paragraph on the left has been expanded into a five-paragraph compare-contrast essay on the right. The highlighted sentences in the essay are the same as or similar to those in the paragraph. Notice that many of the sentences in Paragraph 33 become topic sentences in the essay.

Work with a partner to answer the questions before and after the paragraph and essay. These questions will help you to understand content and organization.

1. What do you know about the weather in Chicago? Miami?

   _____

   _____

2. In your opinion, what is the best weather? Can you think of a place that has what you consider to be the best weather?

   _____

   _____

EXAMPLE PARAGRAPH
Paragraph 33

The Weather in Chicago and Miami

My cousin and I recently had a discussion about whether his hometown, Chicago, or my hometown, Miami, has better weather. Our discussion centered on three differences between the weather in our two hometowns. First, Chicago has all four seasons, but Miami does not. Chicago enjoys summer, fall, winter, and spring weather. Miami, in contrast, has only two seasons: a very mild winter and a very long summer. Another major difference in the weather between our two cities is that Chicago's worst weather occurs in the winter. On average, the high temperature reaches only around 32 degrees and the low each night goes down to about 20 degrees. The problem in Miami is not the cold but rather the heat. In the summer, the temperature reaches 95 degrees in the daytime and drops only to 75 or so at night. Finally, people in each city worry about different weather problems. While a Chicagoan's biggest weather fear is a blizzard, the biggest weather problem for peple in Miami is a hurricane. In the end, my cousin and I learned that each of our hometowns has unique weather.

ESSAY 3

The Weather in Chicago and Miami

Paragraph 34

People usually have very strong opinions about what constitutes good weather, and one person's idea of good weather may easily be another person's weather nightmare. In fact, my cousin and I recently had a discussion about whether his hometown, Chicago, or my hometown, Miami, has better weather. Our discussion centered on three differences between the weather in our two hometowns.

Paragraph 35

Our first point of discussion was the number of seasons. Chicago is located in the Midwestern part of the U.S. It is also much farther north than Miami is. Chicago has four seasons: summer, fall, winter, and spring. These four seasons are clearly marked by distinct weather changes. Miami, on the other hand, is in the southeastern corner of the United States. Because it is much farther south, near the Caribbean and Gulf of Mexico, Miami is much warmer. Miami has two seasons: a very mild winter and a long summer.

Paragraph 36

We also considered the worst temperatures in both cities. The worst weather in Chicago occurs in the winter. On average, the high temperature only reaches around 32 degrees and the low each night goes down to about 20 degrees. In addition, frequent high winds drive the perceived temperature down even more. This combination of cold and wind, called the wind chill factor, can make life almost unbearable in Chicago during the winter months. The problem in Miami is not the cold but rather the heat. In the summer, the temperature reaches 95 degrees in the daytime and drops only to 75 or so at night. Combined with a constant humidity of 90 percent or more, the temperature actually feels significantly warmer.

Paragraph 37

Finally, our two hometowns have different kinds of bad weather. Chicagoans' biggest weather fear is a blizzard. Blizzards can occur frequently during the frigid winter months. When a blizzard hits the city, it can dump up to five or six feet of snow in certain areas. The cold and snow paralyze the city, making it impossible for people to go to school or work. While blizzards affect Chicago, the biggest weather problem for people in Miami is a hurricane. Hurricanes are possible from May through November. While hurricanes occur less frequently than blizzards, they can cause much more damage. For instance, Hurricane Andrew destroyed large parts of the city of Miami in 1992.

Paragraph 38

In the end, my cousin and I learned that each of our climates has its unique characteristics. Chicagoans have to live with extreme cold and frequent blizzards that can upset their daily routines. Conversely, Miami enjoys warm temperatures while having to deal with the threat of hurricanes. Deciding which city has better weather proved to be more difficult than we anticipated. My cousin does not like hot weather, and I can't stand the cold. Thus, we believe that the definition of perfect weather depends largely on each person's preference.

constitutes: equals, makes up

nightmare: a bad dream

in fact: really, truly, for example

centered on: focused on

farther: more distant (far—farther—
the farthest)

distinct: clearly different

mild: not very hot and not very cold

perceived: felt by the senses

unbearable: cannot bear, cannot stand

drops: goes down

humidity: water in the air

significantly: much, considerably

blizzard: a severe winter storm marked by
very strong winds and heavy snowfall

dump: drop, usually in a pile

up to: as much as, as high as

paralyze: cause to be unable to move

hurricane: a severe tropical storm marked
by very strong winds and heavy rainfall

while: although, though (shows contrast)

for instance: for example

destroyed: completely ruined

in the end: the final result

upset: bother, force out of the usual position

daily routine: what we do every day

deal with: handle; cope with

threat: a danger, a potential problem

anticipated: believed possible, expected

stand: tolerate, put up with

largely: mostly

3. What characteristics does the writer compare in this essay?

    _____

4. What method of organization does the writer use: point-by-point or block?

    _____

5. Circle the hook.

6. Underline the thesis statement. Is the thesis restated in the conclusion

    (paragraph 38)? _____ If yes, underline that sentence (or sentences).

7. Supporting sentences: Underline one supporting sentence in each body
    paragraph (Paragraphs 35, 36, and 37).

8. Reread the concluding paragraph. Does the writer offer a **suggestion**, an
    opinion, or a **prediction**? Circle the appropriate word in bold and write the
    sentence from the essay.

    _____

    _____

WRITER'S NOTE: Adverbs of Degree

Adverbs can be adverbs of manner (*quickly, loudly*), time (*now, yesterday*), place (*here, there*), frequency (*always, never*), and degree. Adverbs of degree tell the extent of something. Other common examples include *very, extremely, completely, relatively,* and *nearly*.

In "The Weather in Chicago and Miami," page 103, find the words *significantly* and *largely*, which are adverbs of degree.

Writing Tip: For better writing, try to avoid the overused word *very*. Instead, use other adverbs of degree that will make your writing sound more precise.

Activity 4   **Finding Word Forms in Essays**

Study the word forms below and fill in the missing forms. If you need help, refer to "The Weather in Chicago and Miami," page 103, to find the missing word forms. The first one is done for you.

NOUN	VERB	ADJECTIVE	ADVERB
1. decision	*decide*	decisive	decisively
2. consideration	_____	considerate	considerately
3. _____	add	additional	additionally
4. frequency	frequent	frequent	_____
5. uniqueness	X	_____	uniquely
6. _____	threaten	threatening	threateningly
7. _____	differ	_____	differently
8. perception	_____	perceptive	perceptively

Activity 5	**Brainstorming and Outlining Practice**

In Activity 1, you chose the five best titles for good compare-contrast essays. Choose one title and brainstorm some ideas for the topic. Then with a partner, in a small group, or on your own, develop a general outline for this essay. (You will not write this essay.) Note: For additional practice, repeat this activity with one of the other four titles.

Your topic: _____

Brainstorming Box

Organizational Method: _point-by-point*_____

Outline:

I. Introduction

Thesis statement: _____

_____

II. Point 1: _____

Details: _____

_____

III. Point 2: _____

Details: _____

_____

*For this exercise, we have chosen point-by-point. If you can use this method, then the block method should be relatively easy.

IV. Point 3: _____

    Details: _____

    _____

V. Conclusion

    Concluding statement: _____

    _____

Connectors and Transitions

Study the chart of common comparing and contrasting structures for connectors and transitions.

Comparing	
Within a Sentence	**Between Sentences**
<ul><li>compared to <u>noun</u></li><li>the same noun as</li><li>as <u>adjective / adverb</u> as</li><li>like <u>noun</u></li><li>not only _____ but also _____ (parallel structure needed)</li><li>both _____ and _____ (parallel structure needed)</li><li>also</li><li>S + V, and S + V</li><li>S + V, and S + V, too</li></ul>	<ul><li>In addition, S + V</li><li>Similarly, S + V</li><li>Likewise, S + V</li><li>_____, and _____ (parallel structure needed)</li></ul>

Contrasting	
Within a Sentence	**Between Sentences**
<ul><li>Although / Even though / Though + S + V, S + V</li><li>Unlike <u>noun</u></li><li>Whereas / While + S + V, S + V</li><li>S + V, but S + V (parallel structure needed)</li></ul>	<ul><li>Conversely, S + V</li><li>However, S + V</li><li>On one hand, S + V</li><li>On the other hand, S + V</li><li>In contrast, S + V</li><li>Nevertheless, S + V</li></ul>

Activity 6	Analysis of Connectors and Transitions

Reread the essay "The Weather in Chicago and Miami," page 103. Indicate whether the following connectors and transitions are for comparison or contrast. Then copy the sentences from the essay that contains the connector or transition.

1. also   _____   _____

                             _____

2. conversely   _____   _____

                             _____

3. while   _____   _____

                             _____

4. on the other hand _____ _____

                             _____

LANGUAGE FOCUS 9: Forming the Comparative and Superlative

1. For one-syllable adjectives and two-syllable adjectives ending in *-y*, add *-er* and *-est* to form the comparative and superlative forms. (*cold / colder / coldest, happy / happier / happiest*)

2. Other adjectives are preceded by *more* and *the most* to form the comparative and superlative forms. (*more beautiful / the most beautiful*)

3. Exceptions include *good / better / the best, bad / worse / the worst, far / farther / the farthest*

   I think cake is <u>better</u> than candy, but <u>the best</u> dessert is ice cream.

4. When the items being compared are the same, use *as* + adjective / adverb *as* or *the same* + noun + *as*.

   In my opinion, a Toyota Corolla is <u>as beautiful as</u> a Mercedes even though they are not <u>the same price</u>.

LANGUAGE FOCUS 10: Parallel Structure

1. Words in a list should be the same part of speech. Use three nouns, three adjectives, or three verbs, but do not mix these parts of speech.

    Though New York City in 1900 was quite different from New York City in 2000 in many ways, important similarities existed in <u>population</u>, <u>employment</u>, and <u>transportation</u>. (three nouns)

2. Phrases and clauses in a list should be parallel. Use a prepositional phrase and another prepositional phrase, a noun clause and another noun clause, and so on.

    Survey results can be misleading because there is a huge difference between <u>what people think they do</u> and <u>what people actually do</u>. (two noun clauses)

Activity 7   **Comparatives, Superlatives, and Parallel Structure**

If the underlined part is incorrect, write a correction above it.

1. <u>The most expensive</u> items in this company's budget are employee salaries, communication costs, and <u>supplies that are used in the office</u>.

2. Without a doubt, I think London is <u>interesting</u> to visit than either Cairo or Tokyo.

3. The car was going <u>as fast as</u> the truck was, but the car had an accident because it turned the corner <u>more sharply than</u> the truck.

4. When you are a first-time visitor to a new city, <u>the more important things</u> that you need are a clean place to stay, good food <u>that you can eat</u>, and enough money to get both of these.

5. Some doctors believe that it is <u>most healthy to eat</u> several small meals each day than it is to eat one big meal.

WORKING WITH LANGUAGE IN A COMPARE-CONTRAST ESSAY

Read the whole essay "The Wonder of Flight" (Paragraphs 39–43). Then go back and complete each activity.

Activity 8	Sentence Combining

Use the three pieces of information below the paragraph to compose a sentence that fits in the blank.

Essay 4

EXAMPLE ESSAY

The Wonder of Flight

_____   **Paragraph 39**

_____

Since then, I have always enjoyed the rush and freedom of taking off in my single-engine Cessna and soaring through the sky. Recently, Adam, a friend from high school who shares my appreciation of flight, invited me to come with him to a park to fly his remote-controlled model airplane. I was pleasantly surprised to find that the experience of flying a model plane is remarkably similar to piloting a real plane.

    a. I earned my license.

    b. The license was a pilot's license.

    c. I did this when I was fifteen years old.

Activity 9   **Connectors and Transitions**

Complete the sentences with the connectors and transitions in the box.

both	for example	as	when	both	also

EXAMPLE ESSAY

❶ _____ we arrived at the park, it was interesting to watch my friend   **Paragraph 40**
prepare his model airplane for flight. The procedures that he followed reminded me of
the preflight procedures that I follow each time I fly my Cessna. **❷** _____
model planes and real planes require maintenance to operate them safely.
❸ _____, they **❹** _____ need to be fueled before takeoff. In a
way, a model enthusiast serves as the ground crew for his model aircraft. My friend
must refuel the plane before each flight and do a visual check of the aircraft.
He must **❺** _____ test the flight controls just **❻** _____ a real
pilot checks the flight controls of his or her plane before takeoff.

Activity 10   **Edit from Teacher's Comments**

*Read the paragraph and the teacher's comments. On the basis of these comments, rewrite this
paragraph on the blank lines.*

EXAMPLE ESSAY

          word form
I was (1) <u>fascinating</u> to learn that a model plane operates under the same basic   **Paragraph 41**
              wrong word
physics of flight as my Cessna (2) <u>is</u>. For example, just like my Cessna, Adam's model
         You need passive voice.
plane (3) <u>powers</u> a gas engine, which spins a propeller to create forward power.
                  comma splice!
(4) <u>Just like my Cessna, Adam's model airplane has a wing, it creates lift.</u> This keeps the

model floating in the air. Likewise, both planes use ailerons and flaps to control their
                Fragment!
direction. (5) <u>Surprisingly, even though the model plane is only five feet long.</u> It flies
                   word form
at about eighty miles per hour, which is just twenty miles per hour (6) <u>slow</u> than my
    How is this sentence related to the topic of this paragraph?
Cessna. (7) <u>I like these planes a lot.</u>

_____

_____

_____

_____

_____

_____

_____

_____

_____

_____

Activity 11   Editing for Errors

This paragraph contains seven errors. They are in articles (2), passive voice (1), subject-verb agreement (1), verb tense (2), and word forms (1). Mark these errors and write the corrections above them.

EXAMPLE ESSAY

Although real airplane is controlled from within the cockpit while a model plane is   **Paragraph 42**

controlled with a remote control, fly each of our planes requires a similar technique.

Consequently, because I know how to fly my Cessna, I was easily able to fly the model

plane. Both has a throttle that controls the speed of the plane. Both are using a rudder

on the vertical tail fin that steers the plane left and right while in the air. Also, both

use ailerons on the wings that bank the plane to the left or to the right. Both use wheels

to taxi to the runway on the ground. In fact, in a real plane, the same foot pedals steered

the plane left and right while in the air and guide the plane left and right while on the

ground. Similarly, same left-right motion on the remote control is moved both the

rudder and the wheels.

Activity 12   Using Correct Grammar

Key grammar points are practiced in this paragraph. Underline the correct form in parentheses.

EXAMPLE ESSAY

I was **❶** (delight, delighted) to discover that I can **❷** (experience, to experience) the wonder and thrill of flight **❸** (by, for) flying a model airplane. I had never **❹** (to realize, realized) how **❺** (similar, similarly) model airplanes are **❻** (for, to) real **❼** (airplane, airplanes). Both models and real planes have similar controls. Just like **❽** (real plane, a real plane), Adam's model **❾** (required, requires) preflight maintenance, and **❿** (it operates, they operate) **⓫** (in, on) the same principles of flight as my Cessna. I was glad to share **⓬** (these, this) amazing experience with my friend.

Paragraph 43

Activity 13   Analyzing an Essay

Answer these questions about "The Wonder of Flight," (Paragraphs 39–43).

1. What two things does the writer compare in this essay?

   _____

2. What method of organization does the writer use: point-by-point or block?

   _____

3. What is the hook? Write it here.

   _____

   _____

4. Underline the thesis statement. Is the thesis restated in the conclusion

   (Paragraph 43)? _____ If yes, underline that sentence (or sentences).

5. What is the topic of Paragraph 41? _____

6. Reread the concluding paragraph (Paragraph 43). Does the writer offer a **suggestion**, an **opinion**, or a **prediction**? Circle the appropriate word in bold and write the sentence from the essay.

_____

_____

WRITING A COMPARE-CONTRAST ESSAY

In this section, you will write a compare-contrast essay. Use a separate piece of paper for your work. First, choose a topic from this list:

1. Write about a sports team's (or an athlete's) previous and current performances and records.

2. Compare the cuisine of one country with the cuisine of another country.

3. Compare or contrast the anticipation and expectation of an important event (such as your first date or your first trip on a airplane) with the reality of that event.

4. Compare or contrast two important people that you admire.

5. Compare or contrast two movies of the same type, such as action, science fiction, or romantic comedy.

Then follow Steps 2–8 in Unit 4, pages 91–92, with the following changes:

1. Use a block or a point-by-point outline, modeled on pages 97–98.

2. Use Peer Editing Sheet 9 on page 177 to have your outline checked by a classmate.

3. Use Peer Editing Sheet 10 on page 179 to have your first draft checked by a classmate.

Final Draft Checklist

	Yes	No
1. Did I follow either the block or point-by-point method carefully?		
2. Did I discuss characteristics (block) and/or the subjects for each characteristic (point-by-point) in the same order?		
3. Did I use comparison-contrast connectors and transitions correctly?		
4. Did I use any adverbs of degree correctly?		
5. Is *very* used too often in my essay?		
6. Are all my word forms correct?		
7. Are comparative and superlative forms correct?		
8. Are items in lists parallel?		

ADDITIONAL TOPICS FOR WRITING

Here are five more ideas for writing a compare-contrast essay:

1. Choose one modern convenience such as a cell phone, air conditioning, or fast food and compare life before this was invented and life now.

2. Describe the qualities of two kinds of pets.

3. Compare or contrast shopping at stores and shopping online.

4. Write about two ways to prepare for a big test.

5. Compare or contrast two professions.

Online Study Center   For more practice, go to the *Great Paragraphs to Great Essays* website at http://esl.college.hmco.com/students

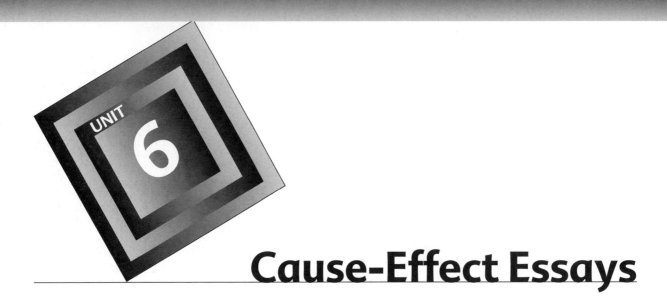

Cause-Effect Essays

Writing Goal:	Writing cause-effect essays
Language Focus 11:	Ways of expressing past actions
Language Focus 12:	Word and preposition combinations
Examples:	Paragraphs 44–56; Essays 5–6

A cause-effect essay serves one of two purposes: Either it shows the effects of a thing or event, or it explains the causes of a thing or event. Cause-effect essays deal with the action/result relationship. They explain why things happen (causes) and what happens as a result (effects). They can be written to inform or to persuade.

CHOOSING A SUBJECT

In a cause-effect essay, it is important to choose a topic that fits a cause-effect relationship. In other words, you need to choose a topic and then describe its causes or its effects. Consider the following charts that show the relationship of causes and effects:

Cause	Effect
Terrorists attacked the United States on September 11, 2001.	It is more difficult for international students to obtain a student visa to study in the United States.
Visibility on the night of March 17, 1977, was poor.	Seven cars were involved in an accident that killed four people.
People are living longer.	Social Security cannot provide the same benefits to everyone.

Causes	Effect
Jim takes good notes in class.	
Jim studies his notes every night.	Jim gets an A on his exam.
Jim participates in class.	

Cause	Effects
People lose faith in their country's currency.	The value of the currency decreases.
	Prices on most goods increase dramatically.
	Exchange rates for the currency decrease in value.

Activity 1   **Choose Appropriate Topics and Titles**

Read these ten essay titles. Put an X next to the five that are most appropriate for a cause-effect essay. Be prepared to defend your choices.

_____ 1. The Causes of War

_____ 2. Why I Decided to Join the Navy

_____ 3. The Beatles: The Greatest Group Ever?

_____ 4. My First Day Working at McDonald's

_____ 5. The Impact of the Death Penalty

_____ 6. East Coast Beaches Versus West Coast Beaches

_____ 7. The Damaging Effects of a Tsunami

_____ 8. Why I Chose to Attend Miami-Dade College

_____ 9. Inside the Oprah Show

_____ 10. A Comparison of Mark Twain's *The Adventures of Tom Sawyer* and *The Adventures of Huckleberry Finn*

ORGANIZATION OF A CAUSE-EFFECT ESSAY

Once you have chosen a topic, you have to decide to write about either the causes of your topic, the effects, or both. Good writers focus on immediate and direct causes or effects. Here is an example of an outline in which the writer looks at the effects of climate on recreational choices and health.

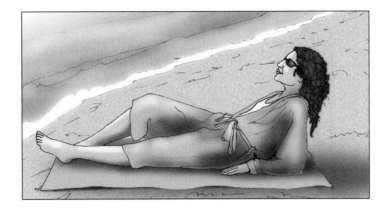

I. Introduction

   A. Hook

   B. Connecting information

   C. Thesis: Sunshine can affect people's moods, choice of activities, and fashion.

II. Mood

   A. Not trapped inside

   B. Increased melatonin production ➔ better mood and sense of well-being

III. Activities

   A. Beach

   B. Picnics

   C. Outdoor sports

IV. Fashion

   A. Lighter-colored clothes

   B. Lighter fabrics, less fabric

V. Conclusion

   A Restatement of thesis

   B. Summary of the main points

NOTE: The conclusion of a cause-effect essay typically restates and summarizes the three points of development (one from each body paragraph).

Supporting Details

In a cause-effect essay, you can organize your supporting details in one of three ways: categorically, chronologically, or in order of importance. In the previous essay outline, the effects of sunshine are organized into three different categories. Now that we have done this, we can fill in the supporting details using concrete examples. It is clear that the writer is trying to show effects of sunlight. By adding specific examples to the existing outline, the essay will be more detailed. Study these examples from Section III of the previous outline.

III. Activities

    A. Beach

        1. Warm water → swimming and surfing

        2. Warm sand → volleyball and looking for shells

    B. Picnics

        1. Socializing

        2. Grilling outdoors

    C. Outdoor sports

        1. Individual sports like golf

        2. Team outdoor sports: soccer, flag football, etc.

Activity 2   Making an Outline for a Cause-Effect Essay

Here is an outline for an essay that discusses the harmful effects of smoking. The outline is missing important pieces. Use the answers below to fill in the missing pieces.

opinion	Hook	Physical/appearance	teeth
unacceptable	Cancer	the main points	Addiction
thesis statement	smokers	Thesis statement	Social

Title: The Harmful Effects of Smoking

   I. Introduction

      A. _____

      B. Connecting information

      C. _____

  II. _____ effects

      A. Stains _____

      B. Causes wrinkles

      C. Causes premature aging

 III. Physiological effects

      A. _____

      B. Exercise is difficult

      C. _____

 IV. _____ effects

      A. Non smokers usually do not socialize with _____

      B. Cannot smoke in many restaurants

      C. Becoming socially _____ (passing of no smoking in restaurants laws)

   V. Conclusion

      A. Restate _____

      B. Summarize _____

      C. Concluding statement: a suggestion, _____, or prediction

Activity 3   Studying a Sample Paragraph to Essay

In both Paragraph 44 and Essay 5, the writer discusses clinical depression. The paragraph on the left has been expanded into a five-paragraph cause-effect essay on the right. The highlighted sentences in the essay are the same as or similar to those in the paragraph. Notice that many of the sentences in Paragraph 44 become topic sentences in the essay.

Work with a partner to answer the questions before and after the paragraph and essay. These questions will help you to understand content and organization.

1. Have you ever been depressed? _____

2. Have you or someone you know ever been diagnosed with clinical depression? If so, what was that experience?

_____

_____

_____

_____

_____

_____

_____

_____

_____

_____

EXAMPLE PARAGRAPH
Paragraph 44

Clinical Depression

People tend to misuse the term depression, using it to refer to the normal ups and downs of daily life, but depression is a serious illness that can be caused by many factors. Perhaps the most common source of depression is genetics. People who are born with low levels of serotonin and dopamine cannot experience pleasure in the same way that balanced people can. These people do not experience happiness from typically happy events. Another cause of depression is alcohol or drug abuse. When drugs enter the bloodstream, they alter the brain's normal chemical balance. Afterward, people who use these chemical substances may experience short-term or long-term depression. Finally, environmental factors can cause clinical depression. Failed relationships, traumatic events, or an abusive childhood can trigger depression. Regardless of its cause, depression is a serious illness that afflicts millions of people throughout the world.

ESSAY 5

Clinical Depression

How many times have you heard the phrase "I am feeling depressed today"? People tend to misuse the term *depression* to refer to the normal ups and downs of daily life. In reality, depression is a serious illness. A clinically depressed person is in a constant state of sadness because of three main factors: genetics, substance abuse, or environment.

Perhaps the most common cause of depression is genetics. People who are born with low levels of serotonin and dopamine in their brains cannot experience pleasure in the same way that balanced people can. As a result, these people do not experience happiness from normal happy events. They require extreme circumstances to experience the same level of happiness that a balanced person would experience from a lesser event. For example, a clinically depressed person might derive less satisfaction from earning an "A" for a course than a balanced person would experience from earning an "A" for an individual assignment.

Another cause of depression is alcohol or drug abuse. When drugs enter the bloodstream, they alter the brain's normal chemical balance. Afterward, people who use these chemical substances may experience short-term or long-term depression due to inadequate levels of these chemicals. As a case in point, an alcoholic can develop depression because of the constant altering of the levels of dopamine in his or her brain. Similarly, when a person uses cocaine, he or she experiences an intense, short-term "high" followed by an equally intense, short-term "low."

Finally, environmental factors can trigger clinical depression. Failed relationships, such as a divorce or a falling out between family members, can leave a person in a state of depression in which the person is unable to handle himself or herself. Traumatic events, such as the death of a family member or the witnessing of a murder, are environmental factors that can send a person into depression. Likewise, an abusive childhood often leads to bouts of clinical depression as an adult.

Depression can be caused by factors such as genetics, substance abuse, or environment. Regardless of its cause, depression is a serious illness that afflicts millions of people throughout the world. Fortunately, it can be treated through various forms of counseling and/or medication, but for this to happen, it is essential that one be able to recognize the symptoms.

Paragraph 45

Paragraph 46

Paragraph 47

Paragraph 48

Paragraph 49

substance abuse: drug/alcohol misuse

environment: surroundings

circumstances: situations

derive: get, obtain

bloodstream: the blood in your body

chemical substances: alcohol, prescription
    drugs, illegal drugs

inadequate: not enough

case in point: an example, for instance

dopamine: a chemical in the brain that
    controls happiness

trigger: cause, start

falling out: serious argument

bouts: short periods

afflicts: affect in a negative manner;
    to bother

counseling: therapy

3. Does the writer tell about causes, effects, or both? _____

4. Underline the hook.

5. Circle the thesis statement. Is the thesis restated in the conclusion
   (Paragraph 49)? If yes, underline that sentence.

6. What are the three main causes of depression?

   a. _____

   b. _____

   c. _____

7. Supporting sentences: In Paragraph 48, the writer writes about environmental
   factors that can cause depression. List those three factors here:

   a. _____

   b. _____

   c. _____

8. How does the writer organize the essay: categorically, chronologically, or order
   of importance?

   _____

Activity 4   Finding Word Forms in Essays

Study the word forms below and fill in the missing forms. If you need help, refer to Essay 5 "Clinical Depression," page 123, to find the missing word forms. The first one is done for you.

NOUN	VERB	ADJECTIVE	ADVERB
1. sadness	sadden	sad	sadly
2. depression	depress	_____	depressingly
3. abuse	_____	abusive	abusively
4. _____	realize	real	really
5. _____	level	level	levelly
6. environment	X	_____	environmentally
7. similarity	X	similar	_____
8. _____	X	genetic	genetically

Activity 5   Brainstorming and Outlining Practice

In Activity 1, you chose the five best titles for good cause-effect essays. Choose one title and brainstorm some ideas for the topic. Use a brainstorming technique from Unit 4, pages 84–85. Then with a partner, in a small group, or on your own, develop a general outline for an essay. (You will not write this essay.) Note: For additional practice, repeat this activity with one of the other four titles.

Your topic: _____

Brainstorming Box

Organizational Method (circle one):   focus on CAUSES   focus on EFFECTS

Supporting details (circle one):   categorical   chronological   order of importance

Outline:

I. Introduction

Thesis statement: _____

_____

II. Cause or effect 1: _____

Details: _____

III. Cause or effect 2: _____

Details: _____

IV. Cause or effect 3: _____

Details: _____

V. Conclusion

Concluding statement: _____

_____

Connectors and Transitions

Study the chart of common cause-and-effect structures.

Comparing	
Within a Sentence	**Between Sentences**
because of + <u>noun</u>	As a result / Therefore / Because of this, S + V
because + S + V	S + V, so S + V
another (cause/effect/reason)	S + V so (that) S + V
owing to + <u>noun</u>	
due to + <u>noun</u>	

Activity 6   **Analysis of Connectors and Transitions**

Reread the essay "Clinical Depression," page 123. Copy the sentences from the essay that contain the connector or transition.

1. due to _____

2. another cause _____

3. as a result _____

4. because of _____

LANGUAGE FOCUS 11: Ways of Expressing Past Actions

Because we often write about events that happened in the past, it is important for good writers to be able to express ideas in the past accurately. Here are four verb tenses that can express past actions.

SIMPLE PAST

Simple past tense uses *-ed* for regular verbs and various forms for irregular verbs. We use the simple past—the most common way of expressing past actions—for an action that is complete.

Because she **worked** so hard, her business **became** very successful.

regular   irregular

PAST PROGRESSIVE

Past progressive tense uses *was* or *were* and the *-ing* form of the verb. We use past progressive tense especially for actions that were interrupted by another (usually shorter) action.

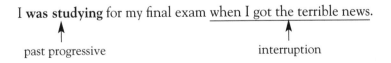

I **was studying** for my final exam <u>when I got the terrible news.</u>

past progressive   interruption

PRESENT PERFECT

Verbs in the present perfect tense consist of *have* or *has* plus the past participle (*gone, lived*). Present perfect can describe two kinds of past actions. One is an action that began in the past and continues now.

These people **have lived** in this area for almost a century.

The second is a past action that is important to the current situation or discussion. This second use is particularly common near the beginning of essays because the present perfect tense helps readers to connect past events with the current situation, which is often the main focus of the essay.

People are angry because the President **has increased** taxes again.

PAST PERFECT

The past perfect tense is formed with *had* and the past participle (*gone, worked*). This verb tense is not so common. In fact, the most common error occurs when writers overuse the past perfect. (*Hint:* If you cannot think of a specific reason to use past perfect, do not use it. Use the simple past instead.) The past perfect is used when there are two past actions and the writer wants to clearly show which one happened first. The earlier action is in past perfect, and the other action is usually expressed in simple past tense.

Dinosaurs **had disappeared** long before humans appeared on the earth.

Activity 7	Practice with Present and Past Tense

Read the following paragraph completely first. Then underline the correct verb tense in parentheses.

Paragraph 50

EXAMPLE PARAGRAPH

One similarity between Brazil and the United States ❶ (is, was, had been) the diversity of ethnic groups. Brazil ❷ (is, was, had been, was being) colonized by Europeans, and its culture has been greatly influenced by this fact. However, the identity of the Brazilian people is not only a product of Western civilization. Brazil ❸ (is, was, had been) a "melting pot" of many ethnic groups that ❹ (were immigrating, immigrated) there and mixed with the native people. The United States also has a diversity of ethnic groups that ❺ (represented, represent, had represented) the early colonists from northern Europe as well as groups from Africa, the Mediterranean, Asia, and South America. The most notable effect of this mixture of cultures and customs ❻ (worked, has worked, was working, had worked) to form ethnically rich cultures in both countries.

LANGUAGE FOCUS 12: Word and Preposition Combinations

Advanced writers use correct word combinations. Study these common combinations.

Common NOUN + PREPOSITION combinations			
cost of	limitations of	source of	lack of
order of	request for	reason for	need for
state of	alternative to	answer to	application for
increase in	decrease in	trouble with	demand for
(have an) effect on	price of	means of	interest in
Common PREPOSITION + NOUN combinations			
in reality	by hand	in order	at every point
for dinner	in general	in the beginning	in a hurry
for sale	in writing	in stock	in other words
on television	for the record	out of order	in fact
under pressure	out of date	with reference to	at the same time

Activity 8   Practice with Word and Preposition Combinations

Underline the preposition that best completes the sentence. If more than one preposition is possible, circle the other possibilities.

Paragraph 51

EXAMPLE PARAGRAPH

I certainly understand that there is a huge need ❶ (at, by, for, with) air conditioning. ❷ (By, With, For, At) the same time, however, I am concerned about the negative effects that air conditioning has had ❸ (at, in, on, with) our lives. To be sure, air conditioning has benefited us, but what has the price ❹ (of, by, with, in) this benefit been? First of all, people do not get outside as much. People tend to stay cooped up inside their air-conditioned homes. As a result, they are not getting as much fresh air. Second, there has been a decrease ❺ (on, in, for) the amount of exercise that people are doing. They do not even walk outside on some days, which means that they are ❻ (at, for, in, to) fact doing a lot less exercising. Finally, the invention of air conditioning has caused us to work longer hours because employers expect us to stay inside our comfortable workspace all day long. In sum, air conditioning might appear to be a positive thing, but it has had at least three negative effects.

WORKING WITH LANGUAGE IN A CAUSE-EFFECT ESSAY

Read the whole essay, "The Benefits of a Healthy Lifestyle" (Paragraphs 52–56) first. Then go back and complete each activity.

Activity 9   Sentence Combining

Use the three pieces of information below the paragraph to compose a sentence that fits in the blank.

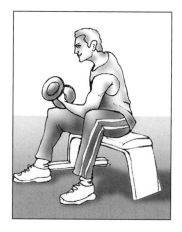

Essay 6

EXAMPLE ESSAY

The Benefits of a Healthy Lifestyle

Paragraph 52

_____

_____

_____ .

Many people are not aware of the effects their diet can have on how they feel. Likewise, they are unaware of the benefits of a regular exercise routine. In fact, there are physical, psychological, and social benefits to living a healthy lifestyle.

  a. There has been a significant increase in the number of obese adults in the United States.

  b. There has been a significant increase in the number of obese children in the United States.

  c. Because of this, people's eating and exercising habits have become regular topics in the media.

Activity 10   **Connectors and Transitions**

Complete the sentences with the connectors and transitions in the box.

Equally beneficial	also	Another
For instance	so that	Thus

Paragraph 53

EXAMPLE PARAGRAPH

A person can reap physical benefits from choosing to follow a healthy lifestyle. ❶ _____, proper exercise and a well-balanced diet help a person to maintain a slim, athletic figure. Countless studies have shown that a regular exercise routine significantly reduces the risk of almost every major disease. Healthy habits ❷ _____ give a person more energy ❸ _____ they can see more, do more, and experience more from life. ❹ _____, people who maintain a healthy lifestyle will, on the average, outlive their unhealthy counterparts. ❺ _____ physical benefit that people notice is healthier-looking skin. ❻ _____, a person can reap many physical benefits from maintaining a healthy lifestyle.

Activity 11   **Edit from Teacher's Comments**

Read the following paragraph and the teacher's comments. On the basis of these comments, rewrite this paragraph on the blank lines.

Paragraph 54

EXAMPLE PARAGRAPH

word form
People who take care of themselves stand to gain psychological (1) beneficial.

Because of the effects their healthy choices have on their bodies, they generally feel
Fragment
better about themselves.(2) While regular exercise produces endorphins, which are

subject-verb agreement
the body's natural mood enhancer. Eating healthy (3) give your body the nutrients it

unclear pronoun reference
needs for radiant skin and strong muscles. (4) They are also better equipped to deal

run-on
with the stress of day-to-day life. (5) Most important, people who take care of

themselves agree that they feel better about themselves because they look better they have

How is this last sentence related to the paragraph?
an increased confidence in themselves. (6) They can lift weights to make them stronger.

_____

_____

_____

_____

_____

_____

_____

_____

_____

_____

Activity 12   Editing for Errors

This paragraph contains six errors. They are in articles (2), subject-verb agreement (1), verb tense (2), and word forms (1). Mark these errors and write the corrections above them.

Paragraph 55

EXAMPLE PARAGRAPH

Taking proper care of one's health also leads to better social life. The confidence a person gains from feeling healthy and in shape improves his or her social and business relationships. Because health-minded people engage in a variety of physical activities, they had increased their chances of meeting people. For example, many people makes friends at the locally gym. Similarly, someone who goes to beach frequently to play volleyball greatly increases his or her chances of meeting a potential romantic partner. Since people who pursue a healthy lifestyle are looking and feel better about themselves, they are more likely to have fulfilling social lives.

Activity 13   Using Correct Grammar

Key grammar points are practiced in this paragraph. Underline the correct form in parentheses.

Paragraph 56

EXAMPLE PARAGRAPH

It certainly ❶ (makes, had made, was making, made) sense ❷ (to, for) live a healthy lifestyle; the benefits ❸ (were, are) clear. Although ❹ (changing, changed) one's eating and exercising patterns may be difficult at first, it becomes easy with time. People ❺ (do not, did not, had not) have to start by changing ❻ (their, his) whole life; they can start by making small changes each day or each week ❼ (until, before) they have transformed themselves. ❽ (While, After) pursuing a ❾ (health, healthy) lifestyle may require a good deal of time and energy, the physical, psychological, and emotional benefits ❿ (are, were, have been, had been) well worth the effort.

Activity 14 — Analyzing the Essay

Answer these questions about "The Benefits of a Healthy Lifestyle" (Paragraphs 52–56).

1. What is the topic of the essay?

   _____

2. Does the writer tell about causes, effects, or both?

   _____

3. Underline the hook.

4. What are the three main effects of living a healthy lifestyle?

   a. _____

   b. _____

   c. _____

5. Underline the thesis statement. Is the thesis restated in the conclusion

   (paragraph 56)? _____ If yes, underline that sentence (or sentences).

6. Supporting sentences: In Paragraph 53, the writer writes about the physical benefits of a healthy lifestyle. List three of the benefits here:

   a. _____

   b. _____

   c. _____

7. How does the writer organize the essay: categorically, chronologically, or order of importance?

   _____

WRITING A CAUSE-EFFECT ESSAY

In this section, you will write a cause-effect essay. Use a separate piece of paper for your work. First, choose a topic from the following list:

1. Discuss the effects of reality television on society.

2. Write about the main causes reasons (causes) that animals become endangered.

3. Discover the causes of war.

4. Tell about the effects of child obesity.

5. Gasoline prices have risen recently. Write about the positive effects of this rise in gasoline prices.

Then follow Steps 2–8 in Unit 4, pages 84–90, with the following changes.

1. Use the outline in Activity 5 on pages 125–126.

2. Use Peer Editing Sheet 11 on page 181 to have your outline checked by a classmate.

3. Use Peer Editing Sheet 12 on page 183 to have your first draft checked by a classmate.

4. In addition to items 1–4 and 7–10 in the Final Draft Checklist in Unit 4, page 93, use the following checklist to review your final draft. Use all the feedback that you have received, including your peer feedback, instructor comments, and self-evaluation. In addition, try reading your essay aloud. When you finish, add a title to your essay.

Final Draft Checklist

	Yes	No
1. Have I assumed a cause-effect relationship when one does not really exist?		
2. Did I use several cause-effect essay transition expressions correctly?		
3. Did I avoid any unnecessary changes in verb tense?		
4. Did I use the past tenses correctly?		
5. Did I use word and preposition combinations correctly?		
6. Does the conclusion restate the main points of development?		

ADDITIONAL TOPICS FOR WRITING

Here are five more ideas for writing a cause-effect essay:

1. Explain the effects of stress on any part of your life.

2. Tell about the effects the invention of e-mail has had on society.

3. Discuss possible reasons (causes) why people mistreat their friends/loved ones.

4. What makes a person successful? (causes)

5. Discuss the positive effects of extra-curricular activities on child development.

 **Online Study Center**   For more practice, go to the *Great Paragraphs to Great Essays* website at http://esl.college.hmco.com/students

Classification Essays

Writing Goal:	Writing Classification Essays
Language Focus 11:	Passive Voice
Language Focus 12:	Adjective Clauses
Examples:	Paragraphs 57–67; Essays 7–8

A well-written classification essay includes all the categories that pertain to the main thing that is being classified. The most important element of a classification essay is its principle of organization. For example, in writing a classification essay on types of movies, a writer can choose which principle of organization to use: genre, period in which the movie was made, audience type, character roles, and so on. Once a writer chooses how to classify the movies, he or she can write a classification essay.

CHOOSING A SUBJECT

Almost any subject can be turned into a classification essay. The key is to select the best **principle of organization**. It is fairly easy to classify cars into price categories: inexpensive, moderate, and expensive. However, such a topic can become a much more interesting essay if the principle of organization is unique. Instead of writing about the prices of cars, a writer can classify cars based on the gas mileage they get or on the types of cars that appeal to young people.

Whatever principle of organization is chosen, the writer must be careful that all types of that category be represented in the essay.

Activity 1   **Appropriate Topics and Titles**

Read these ten essay titles. Put an X next to the five that are most appropriate for a classification essay. Be prepared to defend your choices.

_____ 1. The Effects of Vegetarianism

_____ 2. Varieties of Computer Jobs

_____ 3. The End of the Day

_____ 4. The Many Types of Students

_____ 5. Beautiful Antarctica

_____ 6. An Argument Against Gun Control

_____ 7. The Major Personality Types of Leaders

_____ 8. Lifestyles of the Rich and Famous

_____ 9. How to Live Like a Millionaire

_____ 10. Three Forms of Democracy

ORGANIZATION OF A CLASSIFICATION ESSAY

Organizing a classification essay is fairly easy. If you classify four types of fast-food restaurants, your essay will contain four body paragraphs. Similarly, if you present three main types of computers, your essay will have three body paragraphs. Make sure that each body paragraph contains the same types of supporting details; in other words, the body paragraphs must be parallel.

Here is a classification essay outline on types of writing. Notice how the supporting details (A–C) are parallel in each paragraph.

I. Introduction

   A. Hook

   B. Connecting information

   C. Thesis statement: Most people, at some time in their lives, experience three major types of writing: writing for pleasure, academic writing, and writing in the workplace.

II. Writing for pleasure

   A. Who does it   (detail 1)

   B. When it is done   (detail 2)

   C. What writing tasks are included   (detail 3)

III. Academic writing

   A. Who does it   (detail 1)

   B. When it is done   (detail 2)

   C. What writing tasks are included   (detail 3)

IV. Writing in the workplace

   A. Who does it   (detail 1)

   B. When it is done   (detail 2)

   C. What writing tasks are included   (detail 3)

V. Conclusion

Supporting Details

By adding specific examples to the existing general outline, the essay will be more detailed. Study the supporting details for Section II of the previous outline.

II. Writing for pleasure

   A. Who does it

      1. Adults

      2. Teenagers

      3. Children

B. When it is done

1. During free time (weekends, holidays)

2. Late at night

3. Early in the morning

C. What writing tasks are included

1. Letters

2. Poems

3. Short stories

4. Personal journals

Activity 2 — Making an Outline for a Classification Essay

Here is an outline for an essay that classifies different types of acting. The outline is missing important pieces. Use the answers below to fill in the missing pieces. (If you need help, see Essay 7 on page 144.)

TV acting	Form	Classification #3	Screenplay
Same set	No editing	Cue cards	Introduction
Thesis statement	Memorize lines	Boredom	Stories change every week

Title: The Many Faces of Acting

I. _____

   A. Hook

   B. Background information

   C. _____

II. Classification #1: _____

   A. Form

     1. TV programs

     2. Studio lots

B. Story/set

   1. _____

   2. Writers create new character sets, dialogues, and scenes

C. Actor responsibilities

   1. Actors practice 5–6 days

   2. Shooting on the last day

D. Advantages

   1. _____

   2. Director's help

   3. Taped until it is just right

E. Tie-up sentence

III. Classification #2: stage acting

A. _____

   1. Shakespeare's plays on stage

   2. Modern plays on stage

B. Story/set

   1. Stories are repeated

   2. _____

C. Actor responsibilities

   1. Study for months

   2. Importance of understudies

D. Disadvantages

   1. _____

   2. Great one day; terrible the next

IV. _____ : Film acting

   A. Form

      1. _____

      2. Becomes a movie

   B. Story/set

      1. On location

      2. Beginning, middle, and end

   C. Actor responsibilities

      1. _____

      2. Do not study in chronological order

   D. Advantages or disadvantages

      1. Repeat scenes (advantage)

      2. _____ (disadvantage)

V. Conclusion

   A. Restate the thesis statement

   B. Summarize the main points

   C. Concluding statement: a suggestion, opinion, or prediction

---

Activity 3   **Studying a Sample Paragraph to Essay**

In both Paragraph 57 and Essay 7 on page 144, the writer discusses different kinds of acting. The paragraph on the left has been expanded into a five-paragraph classification essay on the right. The highlighted sentences in the essay are the same as or similar to those from the paragraph. Notice that many of the sentences in Paragraph 57 become topic sentences in the essay.

Work with a partner to answer the questions before and after the paragraph and essay. These questions will help you to understand content and organization.

1. Have you ever acted in front of an audience?

_____

_____

_____

_____

2. Do think that acting is hard work? Why or why not?

_____

_____

_____

_____

EXAMPLE PARAGRAPH
Paragraph 57

The Many Faces of Acting

Modern acting comes in a variety of forms and can be classified in three ways: television acting, stage acting, and film acting. Perhaps the best-known type of acting is television acting. This type of acting generally takes the form of television programs produced on studio lots. Another form of acting is stage acting. In stage acting, the same performance is repeated, and the sets stay the same for each performance. The shows are performed in places ranging from large halls to small theaters. Finally, there is film acting. Film acting begins with a screenplay, which includes all the written information about the set and the actors' dialogues and grows into a movie. Whichever form it takes—television, stage, or film—acting is a form of entertainment that many people enjoy.

ESSAY 7

The Many Faces of Acting

Acting has been a form of entertainment for millennia. Through the years, it has evolved to serve a global audience. As recently as a few generations ago, the most common form of acting was found on radio programs. During this time, listeners had to imagine the sets, the scenery, and even the physical form of the performers. Nowadays, it is difficult to imagine acting as a form of entertainment without visual stimulation. Modern acting comes in a variety of forms. Still keeping some of its roots from Greek times, acting can be classified in three ways: television acting, stage acting, and film acting.

Perhaps the best-known type of acting is television acting. This type of acting generally takes the form of television programs produced on studio lots. The story lines change from week to week as writers create new sets, dialogues, and scenes for the main characters. Performers come to work five days a week to practice their lines. On the final day, the TV cameras are turned on and shooting begins. TV actors have the help of cue cards and off-camera directors who can help them to deliver their lines. Television scenes can be taped repeatedly until the actors get it just right. With TVs in practically every household, it is no wonder this is the most common form of acting.

Another form of acting is stage acting. Plays, ranging from Shakespearean classics to modern tales, can be performed in places ranging from large halls or small theaters. In stage acting, the same performance is repeated, and the sets stay the same for each performance. Rehearsing for stage acting can take months because all the actors must memorize their lines. In addition, stage acting is "live," so the use of understudies—or replacement actors—is crucial. If the star of a stage play is injured or cannot perform, the understudy fills in. Because there is no way to edit the performance, stage performances can be excellent one day and terrible the next. Many people say that there is nothing more entertaining than watching actors performing live on the stage.

Finally, there is film acting. Film acting begins with a screenplay, which includes all the written information about the set and the actors' dialogues and grows into a movie. It can occur anywhere in the world. For instance, if the story line of a film happens to take place in Russia, the film crew and actors can go on location in that country to film. While screenplays have a beginning, a middle, and an end, the filming of movies does not have to be in chronological order. That is, actors may memorize their lines for the ending of the movie and film those scenes before working on the beginning. Because it is not a live performance, directors may request that an actor repeat a scene until the director is happy with the results. This can lead to boredom on the part of the actor.

Whichever form it takes—television, stage, or film—acting as a form of entertainment ranks very high on most people's lists of favorite activities to watch. Still, it is interesting to note that different forms of acting have unique characteristics. Regardless of the type of acting one enjoys, it is safe to say that the audience appreciates the craft of acting and the many hours of enjoyment it provides.

Paragraph 58

Paragraph 59

Paragraph 60

Paragraph 61

Paragraph 62

millennia: thousands of years

shooting: filming

cue: a word or signal marking the moment for an actor to speak

get it: perform

practically: almost

no wonder: not surprising

ranging: extending; going

rehearsing: practicing

that is: specifically; to be exact

boredom: dullness; lacking excitement

ranks: classifies (usually by some type of hierarchy)

regardless: no matter what; despite

craft: skill; expertise

3. What principle of organization does the writer use to classify acting? (Circle one.)

   a. genre (comedy, drama, etc.)

   b. visual form

   c. type of acting

   d. cost

4. Circle the hook.

5. Underline the thesis statement. Is the thesis restated in the conclusion (the fifth paragraph)? If so, underline that sentence (or sentences).

6. Supporting sentences: In Paragraph 59, the author writes about the duties of TV writers. What three things are they responsible for creating?

   a. _____

   b. _____

   c. _____

7. Which paragraph talks about actors getting bored? _____

Explain why these types of actors might get bored while acting.

_____

_____

8. Reread the concluding paragraph of Essay 7. Does the writer offer a **suggestion**, an **opinion**, or a **prediction**? Circle the appropriate word in bold and write the sentence from the essay.

_____

_____

_____

Activity 4	Finding Word Forms in Essays

Study the word forms below and fill in the missing forms. If you need help, refer to the essay "The Many Faces of Acting," page 144, to find the missing word forms. The first one is done for you.

NOUN	VERB	ADJECTIVE	ADVERB
1. evolution	evolve	evolving/evolved	X
2. delivery	_____	delivered	X
3. repetition	repeat	repetitive	_____
4. entertainment	entertain	_____	entertainingly
5. chronology	X	_____	chronologically
6. _____	bore	boring/bored	boringly/boredly
7. rank	_____	ranked	X
8. appreciation	_____	appreciative	appreciatively

Activity 5	Brainstorming and Outlining Practice

In Activity 1, you chose the five best titles for good classification essays. Choose one title and brainstorm some ideas for the topic. Use the brainstorming techniques from Unit 4, pages 84–85. Then with a partner, in a small group, or on your own, develop a general outline for an essay. (You will not write this essay.) Note: For additional practice, repeat this activity with one of the other four titles.

Your topic: _____

Brainstorming Box

Principle of organization: _____

Outline:

  I. Introduction

     Thesis statement: _____

     _____

 II. Type 1: _____

     Details: _____

III. Type 2: _____

     Details: _____

IV. Type 3: _____

     Details: _____

 V. Conclusion

     Concluding statement: _____

     _____

Connectors and Transitions

Study the chart of common connectors and transitions and their functions (in parentheses) to use in classification essays.

Listing and Giving Examples	
Within a Sentence	**Between Sentences**
this type of <u>noun</u>, (classifying) another <u>noun</u> (listing)	In addition, (giving additional information) For instance, (giving an example) Finally, S + V (giving the last example)

Relationship	
Within a Sentence	**Between Sentences**
during + <u>noun</u> (time relationship) before + <u>present participle</u> (time relationship) regardless of + <u>noun</u> (contrasting) if + <u>noun</u> + verb (condition)	That is, S + V (restating) Still, S + V (contrasting)

Activity 6 — Analysis of Connectors and Transitions

Reread the essay "The Many Faces of Acting" on page 144. Find the connectors and transition words listed below. Fill in the missing information from the sentence. Then write the function of the phrase. (Hint: Use the chart above for help.)

1. "This type _____."

   Function: _____

2. "For instance, _____."

   Function: _____

3. "Another _____."

   Function: _____

4. "During _____."

    Function: _____

5. "That is, _____."

    Function: _____

LANGUAGE FOCUS 13: Passive Voice

In passive voice, the subject (agent) of the sentence becomes the receiver of the action. Study these four steps in forming the passive voice.

Step 1: Switch the subject and the object.

Active voice: **Billy** broke his new **baseball bat.**

Passive voice: The new **baseball bat** was broken by **Billy.**

Step 2: Add a form of the verb "to be." Keep the verb tense of the original active voice verb.

Active voice: Billy broke his new baseball bat.

Passive voice: The new baseball bat **was** broken by Billy.

Step 3: Change the main verb in the active voice sentence to the past participle in the passive voice.

Active voice: Billy **broke** his new baseball bat.

Passive voice: The new baseball bat was **broken** by Billy.

Step 4: Add the preposition "by" to show who performed the action. (This step is optional.)

Active voice: Billy broke his new baseball bat.

Passive voice: The new baseball bat was broken **by** Billy.

NOTE: In English, the most important information, the subject, is generally placed at the beginning of a sentence. This noun or pronoun is usually the doer of the action, which results in a subject-verb-object sentence. However, when the receiver of the action (rather than the doer) becomes the main focus of attention, then we use passive voice. Thus, passive voice is used to put more emphasis on the receiver of the action than on the subject (agent).

WRITER'S NOTE: Using Passive Voice

Though passive voice is a correct English sentence construction, some writers use passive voice too much. Writers should use passive voice only when it is necessary. If you have three consecutive sentences with passive voice, it is almost always a good idea to revise one or more of them to be active.

Language Focus 14: Adjective Clauses

Adjective clauses are used to combine two ideas (simple sentences) into one complex sentence. Study the following rules and examples:

1. Adjective clauses must contain a subject and a verb.

2. The subject of an adjective clause can be *who* (people), *which* (things), or *that* (people or things).

   Joann lived in a city. The city was polluted.

   Joann lived in a city **which was polluted.**

   > NOTE: If the information in the adjective clause is necessary to clarify who or what, do not use a comma to separate the ideas.

   My brother wants to climb Mount Everest. He is athletic.

   My brother, **who is athletic**, wants to climb Mount Everest.

   > NOTE: If the information in the adjective clause is not necessary to understand the meaning of the sentence, use a comma to separate the adjective clause from the rest of the sentence.

| Activity 7 | Practice with Passive Voice and Adjective Clauses |

If the underlined part is incorrect, write a correction above it.

1. My car <u>was drive</u> by my mother, and now the steering wheel <u>is not working</u> properly.

2. Everyone likes the professor <u>which teaches</u> the introduction to psychology course.

3. Oil <u>is produced</u> mainly in the Middle East, but Venezuela, <u>which lies</u> in South America, also produces it.

4. How many times have you eaten in the Italian restaurant <u>who is located</u> downtown?

5. The exam <u>that we took</u> last week was very easy. I am not sure that it <u>was written</u> by my teacher!

6. The skills that are needed by modern soldiers <u>cannot be taught</u> in a six-week crash course before <u>these soldiers shipped</u> to a war zone.

7. Before we continue the discussion <u>that we had to leave open yesterday</u>, let me begin today by explaining that pain is really something <u>is felt</u> in your brain.

8. The Cincinnati Zoo & Botanical Garden <u>was rated</u> the #1 attraction in Cincinnati and one of the top five zoos in the nation in a Zagat Survey <u>that conducted</u> last year.

WORKING WITH LANGUAGE IN A CLASSIFICATION ESSAY

Read the whole essay, "Vacations for Everyone" (Paragraphs 63–67) first. Then go back and complete each activity.

Activity 8	Sentence Combining

Use the three pieces of information below the paragraph to compose a sentence that fits in the blank.

Essay 8

Vacations for Everyone

On hearing the word *vacation*, most people react positively. _____   **Paragraph 63**

_____

_____ .

Prospective travelers spend hours if not days researching their travel destination. While the destination has a lot to do with the success of a trip, there are other factors to consider. Seasoned travelers will argue that more important than *where* they go on vacation is *who* they go on vacation with. Vacations can be classified on the basis of travel partners. Vacationers can choose to travel with family, with friends, or alone.

A. It can be a long weekend.

B. It can be a spontaneous getaway.

C. It can be a trip around the world.

Activity 9   **Connectors and Transitions**

Complete the sentences with the connectors and transitions from the box.

That is	Finally	For instance
If	Another	

Paragraph 64

Family travel is special. The success of a trip often depends on the relationship that the family members have with one another. ❶ _____ two brothers do not get along at home, chances are that they will fight during the vacation. ❷ _____ potential problem is transportation. ❸ _____, it is much cheaper for a family of four to travel by car than to buy four plane tickets. ❹ _____, finding common sights of interest may be more complicated with family groups. ❺ _____, Dad might want to see the alligator farm while Mom wants to go shopping and the kids are looking for a video arcade. Whatever the problems, a family vacation usually does not change family relationships.

Activity 10   **Edit from Teacher's Comments**

Read the paragraph and the teacher's comments. On the basis of these comments, rewrite this paragraph on the blank lines.

Paragraph 65

Traveling with friends can be an unforgettable experience. Close friends often have

similar personalities, so there will probably not be a lot of fighting during the trip.
How is this sentence related to the topic?   **fragment**
(1) Fighting is dangerous, especially in foreign countries. (2) Because each person is

paying for himself. Transportation costs tend to be lower as well. Good friends
wrong word
(3) which know how to negotiate each other's needs can also avoid fighting over what
                                                                      not parallel
to see. Basically, the closer the friendship, the (4) easy it is to decide on travel

itineraries. If friends are close, even a terrible trip will not ruin the friendship. (5)
wrong transition
However, some friends bond even more when they experience travel emergencies
                          passive voice   **word form**
together. A special closeness (6) is create during the trip. They share both the (7) well

and the bad memories.

_____

_____

_____

_____

_____

_____

_____

_____

_____

_____

Activity 11   Editing for Errors

This paragraph contains seven errors. They are in articles (2), passive voice (1), subject-verb agreement (1), verb form (1), parallelism (1), and word forms (1). Mark these errors and write the corrections above them.

Paragraph 66

Finally, people can choose to travel alone. It takes special person to feel comfortable doing this. This type of individual feel comfortable being alone and having limited company. As for transportation, single travelers are often a luckiest travelers. They have more chances of getting plane seats on stand-by, and sometimes their seats are upgrade to first class. This would be impossible to do with a larger group. Sightseeing is also not a problem for single travelers. They can choose to wake up late in the day, sightsee at night, or skip lunch if they feel like it. Conversely, they might experience feelings of lonely in not being able to talk to someone else about the wonderful things they are seeing and do. Traveling alone can have other benefits as well. Single travelers are more likely to meet others while on vacation. They do not have anyone else to worry about, so they are free to strike up conversations with strangers. Many single travelers loves the solitary adventure and say that they learn a lot about themselves while traveling.

Activity 12 — Using Correct Grammar

Key grammar points are practiced in this paragraph. Underline the correct form in parentheses.

Paragraph 67

Different **1** (form, forms) of travel are available to everyone. **2** (Person, People) **3** (who, which) are comfortable with relatives enjoy family outings and **4** (vacation, vacations). People who **5** (wants, want) to be sure to have the best time possible while avoiding petty arguments travel with **6** (his, their) closest friends. People who **7** (solitary, are solitary) but love the excitement of seeing new places **8** (choose, are chosen) to travel alone. Whatever the personality, there is a travel **9** (choose, choice) for **10** (every people, everyone).

Activity 13 — Analyzing the Essay

Answer these questions about "Vacations for Everyone" (Paragraphs 63–67).

1. What specific subject does the writer classify in this essay?

_____

2. What principle of organization does the writer use: price, travel companions, or destination?

_____

3. Underline the hook.

4. Circle the thesis statement. Is the thesis restated in the conclusion (Paragraph 63)? If so, underline that sentence (or sentences).

5. What is the topic of Paragraph 65?

_____

6. Reread the concluding paragraph. Does the writer offer a **suggestion**, an **opinion**, or a **prediction**? Circle the appropriate word in bold and write the sentence from the essay.

_____

_____

WRITING A CLASSIFICATION ESSAY

In this section you will write a classification essay. Use a separate piece of paper for your work. First, choose a topic from this list:

1. Classify jobs by type.

2. Write about three study techniques.

3. Classify clothing for different occasions and places.

4. Classify a specific type of music into three or four subcategories.

Then follow Steps 2–8 in Unit 4, pages 84–90, with the following changes:

1. Use the outline in Activity 5 on page 147.

2. Use Peer Editing Sheet 13 on page 185 to have your outline checked by a classmate.

3. Use Peer Editing Sheet 14 on page 187 to have your first draft checked by a classmate.

4. In addition to items 1–4 and 7–10 in the Final Draft Checklist in Unit 4, page 93, use the following checklist to review your final draft. Use all the feedback that you have received, including your peer feedback, instructor comments, and self-evaluation. In addition, try reading your essay aloud. When you finish, add a title to your essay.

Final Draft Checklist

	Yes	No
1. Is this clearly a classification essay?		
2. Is my principle of organization easy to understand?		
3. Do all examples of this subject fit into one of the categories listed?		
4. Did I use classification transition expressions correctly?		
5. Are supporting details in the paragraphs parallel?		

ADDITIONAL TOPICS FOR WRITING

Here are five more ideas for writing a classification essay:

1. Classify pets into three distinct categories.

2. Classify different college courses that are available to students.

3. Write about different types of fast-food restaurants.

4. Classify parenting styles.

5. Write an essay classifying tourist attractions.

 **Online Study Center**   For more practice, go to the *Great Paragraphs to Great Essays* website at http://esl.college.hmco.com/students

APPENDIX

Peer Editing Sheets

PEER EDITING SHEET #1

**UNIT 1, Activity 21, page 27
Paragraph**

Writer: _____ Date: _____

Peer editor: _____

1. Does the paragraph have a clear topic sentence?   Yes   No

2. Does the topic sentence have a controlling idea?   Yes   No

3. Does the paragraph have clear supporting sentences?   Yes   No

4. Does each supporting sentence relate to the topic and the
   controlling idea?   Yes   No

5. Is the paragraph indented?   Yes   No

6. Does the paragraph talk about one idea?   Yes   No

7. Does the paragraph have a concluding sentence that restates
   the main idea or brings the paragraph to a logical conclusion?   Yes   No

8. Is there anything in the paragraph that is not clear to you? If so, write it here.

   _____

   _____

9. What is one additional piece of information that you would like to know?

   _____

   _____

PEER EDITING SHEET #2

**UNIT 2, Activity 16, page 49
Paragraph**

Writer: _____ Date: _____

Peer editor: _____

1. What is the general topic of the paragraph? _____

   Write the topic sentence here: _____

   _____

2. What is the general topic of the paragraph? _____

3. Is the writing formal or informal? _____ Does this style suit the topic and audience?

   If not, why not? _____

   _____

Comment as specifically as possible about questions 4–6. Use space on the back if necessary.

4. Does the paragraph have unity? _____

   _____

5. Does the paragraph have coherence? _____

   _____

6. Does the paragraph maintain clarity? _____

   _____

7. Circle the concluding sentence. Do you think it is a good concluding sentence?

   If not, how would you improve it? _____

   _____

PEER EDITING SHEET #3   **UNIT 3, Activity 3, page 55**
Descriptive Paragraph

Writer: _____ Date: _____

Peer editor: _____

1. Does the paragraph have a clear topic sentence?	Yes	No
2. Does the topic sentence have a controlling idea?	Yes	No
3. Does the paragraph have clear supporting sentences?	Yes	No
4. Does each supporting sentence relate to the topic and controlling idea?	Yes	No
5. Is the paragraph indented?	Yes	No
6. Does the paragraph talk about one idea?	Yes	No
7. Does the paragraph have a concluding sentence that restates the main idea or brings the paragraph to a logical conclusion?	Yes	No
8. Does the writer effectively appeal to the reader's senses?	Yes	No
9. Is the paragraph clear and easy to follow?	Yes	No
10. Is the level of writing appropriate for the audience?	Yes	No
11. Does the paragraph stay consistent with respect to person?	Yes	No
12. Does the paragraph effectively accomplish its purpose?	Yes	No
13. Does the paragraph have unity?	Yes	No
14. Does the paragraph have coherence?	Yes	No
15. Do the words and sentences maintain clarity?	Yes	No

PEER EDITING SHEET #4

UNIT 3, Activity 6, page 60
Compare-Contrast Paragraph

Writer: _____ Date: _____

Peer editor: _____

1. Does the paragraph have a clear topic sentence?	Yes	No
2. Does the topic sentence have a controlling idea?	Yes	No
3. Does the paragraph have clear supporting sentences?	Yes	No
4. Does each supporting sentence relate to the topic and controlling idea?	Yes	No
5. Is the paragraph indented?	Yes	No
6. Does the paragraph talk about one idea?	Yes	No
7. Does the writer stick to only comparing or only contrasting?	Yes	No
8. Is the concluding sentence one of these types: restatement, suggestion, opinion, prediction?	Yes	No
9. Is the paragraph clear and easy to follow?	Yes	No
10. Is the level of writing appropriate for the audience?	Yes	No
11. Does the paragraph stay consistent with respect to person?	Yes	No
12. Does the paragraph effectively accomplish its purpose?	Yes	No
13. Does the paragraph have unity?	Yes	No
14. Does the paragraph have coherence?	Yes	No
15. Do the words and sentences maintain clarity?	Yes	No

**UNIT 3, Activity 11, page 66
Cause-Effect Paragraph**

Writer: _____ Date: _____

Peer editor: _____

1. Does the paragraph have a clear topic sentence?   Yes   No

2. Does the topic sentence have a controlling idea?   Yes   No

3. Does the paragraph have clear supporting sentences?   Yes   No

4. Does each supporting sentence relate to the topic and controlling idea?   Yes   No

5. Does the paragraph talk about one idea?   Yes   No

6. Does the paragraph have a concluding sentence that restates the
    main idea or brings the paragraph to a logical conclusion?   Yes   No

7. Does the topic have a real cause-effect relationship?   Yes   No

    Circle the focus of the paragraph: focus on causes   focus on effects

8. Is the paragraph clear and easy to follow?   Yes   No

9. Is the level of writing appropriate for the audience?   Yes   No

10. Does the paragraph stay consistent with respect to person?   Yes   No

11. Does the paragraph effectively accomplish its purpose?   Yes   No

12. Does the paragraph have unity?   Yes   No

13. Does the paragraph have coherence?   Yes   No

14. Do the words and sentences maintain clarity?   Yes   No

PEER EDITING SHEET #6   **UNIT 3, Activity 14, page 70**
                            Classification Paragraph

Writer: _____ Date: _____

Peer editor: _____

1. Does the paragraph have a clear topic sentence?	Yes	No
2. Does the topic sentence have a controlling ideas?	Yes	No
3. Does the paragraph have clear supporting sentences?	Yes	No
4. Does each supporting sentence relate to the topic and controlling ideas?	Yes	No
5. Does the paragraph talk about one idea?	Yes	No
6. Does the paragraph have a concluding sentence that brings the paragraph to a logical conclusion?	Yes	No

7. (Circle a or b) Does the writer

   (a) show different types or categories or

   (b) differentiate between the parts of something?

8. Does the writer classify without overlap between groups?	Yes	No
9. Is the paragraph clear and easy to follow?	Yes	No
10. Is the level of writing appropriate for the audience?	Yes	No
11. Does the paragraph stay consistent with respect to person?	Yes	No
12. Does the paragraph effectively accomplish its purpose?	Yes	No
13. Does the paragraph have unity?	Yes	No
14. Does the paragraph have coherence?	Yes	No
15. Do the words and sentences maintain clarity?	Yes	No

Copyright © Houghton Mifflin Company. All rights reserved.

UNIT 4, Activity 8, Step 6, page 92
Descriptive Essay Outline

Writer: _____ Date: _____

Peer editor: _____

1. What is being described in the outline? _____

2. Is the hook interesting? _____ If not, how could it be made more interesting? _____

   _____

3. What is the general impression that the reader will get from reading this description?

   _____

4. What is being described in the topic sentences?

   Paragraph 2: _____

   Paragraph 3: _____

   Paragraph 4: _____

5. Are the supporting details related to the topic sentence? If not, what changes should be made?

   _____

6. How will the writer end the essay? _____

7. Do you think the essay will be interesting? _____ Write any additional suggestions here.

   _____

   _____

PEER EDITING SHEET #8   **UNIT 4, Activity 11, page 94**
Descriptive Essay

Writer: _____   Date: _____

Peer editor: _____   Essay title: _____

1. In a few words, what is the essay about? _____

   _____

2. Read body paragraphs 2, 3, and 4. Underline all the descriptive adjectives. Which paragraph has

   the most descriptive adjectives? _____ Can you think of two new descriptive adjectives that

   could be added to the essay? (1) _____ (2) _____

   Now write these in the essay where they would be the most effective.

3. Does the writer use more than one sense to help the reader experience the event instead of just

   telling? _____ Which sense does the writer address the most? _____

4. What suggestions or changes would you make for a more descriptive essay?

   _____

   _____

5. What general impression does the reader take away from this essay? _____

   _____

   _____

6. Is the conclusion successful? Why or why not? _____

   _____

   _____

PEER EDITING SHEET #9   **UNIT 5, page 114**
                          Compare-Contrast Essay Outline

Writer: _____   Date: _____

Peer editor: _____   Topic: _____

1. Is the thesis statement clear? _____ If not, make suggestions for changes. _____

   _____

   _____

2. Do these two subjects have enough similarities and/or differences for a good comparison

   essay? _____ If not, why not? _____

   _____

   _____

3. Does each paragraph topic for development clearly state the point of comparison? _____

   If not, make suggestions for improvement. _____

   _____

   _____

4. The best part of the outline is: _____

   _____

   _____

5. Questions I still have about the outline are: _____

   _____

   _____

UNIT 5, page 114
Compare-Contrast Essay

Writer: _____   Date: _____

Peer editor: _____   Essay title: _____

1. In a few words, what is the essay about? _____

    _____

2. Identify the hook. Is it effective? _____ Make any suggestions here. _____

    _____

    _____

3. Does each body paragraph contain a clear topic sentence? _____ If not, underline any
    sections that need improvement.

4. What method of organization does the writer use: block or point-by-point? _____

5. List the main points that the writer compares. _____

    _____

    _____

6. Do the supporting details give examples? (Ask *who? what? where? when? why? how?* about the
    topic sentence) If not, put a star (*) next to the places that need more supporting information.

7. Does the writer use connectors correctly? _____ If not, circle any incorrect connectors or
    any places that need connectors.

8. Does the writer restate the thesis in the conclusion? _____ If not, bring this to the writer's
    attention.

PEER EDITING SHEET #11   **UNIT 6, page 135**
                         Cause-Effect Essay Outline

Writer: _____   Date: _____

Peer editor: _____   Topic: _____

1. What kind of essay will this be: cause or effect? _____ Can you tell this from

   the thesis statement? _____ If not, what changes can you suggest to make the purpose of the

   essay clearer? _____

   _____

2. How many body paragraphs are there? _____ Is each topic for development related to the

   thesis? _____ If not, mark the topics that you think need more work.

3. Do the supporting details relate to the topic sentence? _____ If not, write any suggestions

   that you have here. _____

   _____

4. How are the supporting details organized: categorically, chronologically, or in order of importance?

   _____

5. The best part of the outline is: _____

   _____

6. Questions I still have about the outline are: _____

   _____

   _____

PEER EDITING SHEET #12   **UNIT 6, page 135**
Cause-Effect Essay

Writer: _____   Date: _____

Peer editor: _____   Essay title: _____

1. In a few words, what is the essay about? _____

_____

2. Reread the introductory paragraph. Do the ideas progress smoothly from the hook to the thesis

statement? _____ If not, what suggestions for changes would you make? _____

_____

_____

3. Do all the topic sentences support the thesis statement? _____ Mark any that do not and

write the reason for your opinion. _____

_____

_____

4. Look at the supporting details in each paragraph. Are they related to the topic sentence? _____
If not, underline the details that need revision.

5. Check the connectors in the essay. Is it easy to understand the connection between the causes
and effects? If not, what is missing or needs to be changed?

_____

_____

_____

_____

UNIT 7, page 156
Classification Essay Outline

Writer: _____   Date: _____

Peer editor: _____   Topic: _____

1. Is this topic appropriate for a classification essay? _____ If not, can you make suggestions

    for change? _____

    _____

    _____

2. Is the thesis statement clear? _____ If not, make suggestions for changes. _____

    _____

    _____

3. What principle of organization does the writer use to classify the topic? _____

    _____

4. What is the topic for paragraph 3? _____

5. Now look at the details listed in the outline for paragraph 3. Do you think these are sufficient to

    develop a good paragraph? _____ Can you think of any other details that should be added?

    _____

6. The best part of the outline is: _____

    _____

7. Questions I still have about the outline are: _____

    _____

    _____

UNIT 7, page 156
Classification Essay

Writer: _____ Date: _____

Peer editor: _____ Essay title: _____

1. In a few words, what is the essay about? _____

   _____

2. Identify the hook. Is it effective? _____ Make any suggestions here. _____

   _____

   _____

3. Does each body paragraph contain a clear topic sentence? _____ If not, underline any
   sections that need improvement.

4. How did the writer organize the essay? _____ List the main categories or classifications that

   the writer uses. _____

   _____

5. Does the writer use connectors correctly? _____ If not, circle any incorrect connectors or
   any places that need connectors.

6. Are the supporting details parallel in each body paragraph? If not, make suggestions for

   improvement. _____

   _____

   _____

   _____

Index

189